Afghans
To Treasure

HOUSE of
WHITE
BIRCHES
PUBLISHERS
SINCE 1947

Afghans To Treasure

Printed in the United States of America
First Printing: 1995
Library of Congress Number: 94-79282
ISBN: 1-882138-09-0

Editorial Director: Vivian Rothe
Editor: Carolyn Brooks Christmas
Designers: Minette Collins Smith, Shaun M. Venish
Photographers: Tammy Christian, Rhonda K. Davis, Nora Elsesser
Photo Assistant: Linda Quinlan
Cover Photo: Tammy Cromer-Campbell, Mary Craft

Production Director: Ange Workman
Production Manager: Glenda Chamberlain
Production Artist: Debby Keel
Technical Manager/Production: Vicki Macy
Production Coordinator: Sandra Ridgway
Production Assistants: Cheryl S. Lynch, Cathy Reef

Publishers: Carl H. Muselman, Arthur K. Muselman
Chief Executive Officer: John Robinson
Marketing Director: Scott Moss

Note: We have made every effort to ensure the accuracy and com-
pleteness of the instructions in this book. However, we cannot
be responsible for human error or for the results when using materials
other than those specified in the instructions, or for variations
in individual work.

Cover project: See page 16

elebrate your love of crochet by treating yourself to these delightful afghan designs! Brighten your living room with a selection from the "Perennial Garden" or "Comforts of Home" sections, or add grace and beauty to a bedroom or Victorian parlor with one of the delicate beauties from the "Touch of Romance" section. Create a gift for everyone on your gift list from the new baby to grandparents — everyone loves cozy, cuddly afghans. And you'll love making each one of these designs following the easy instructions and diagrams.

Contents

A Touch of Romance

Draped over a chair, bed or settee, these afghans bring a touch of old-fashioned charm and grace to any room. Choose a design that's simply a fluff of lace to use when only a whisper of warmth is needed, or select a comfortable, cozy cross-stitched floral tapestry design. Romantic afghans can be created to fit every decor, from country to traditional to Victorian, the most romantic of all.

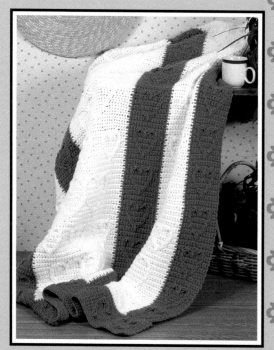

A clever interpretation of a traditional quilt pattern in elegant filet crochet,
this shell-edged afghan is a wonderful idea for a family wedding gift.

Double Wedding Ring

By
KATHERINE ENG

Skill Level
Average

Size
55" x 71"

Materials
4-ply worsted-weight yarn: 49 oz. tan,
2½ oz. off-white, 2½ oz. light coral
Crochet hook size F/5 (4.00mm)

Gauge
4 dc = 1"; 2 dc rows = 1"

Instructions

Notes: *All graph rows may be read left to right. Ch-3 at the beginning of a row counts as 1 dc. Ch-5 at the beginning of a row counts as (1 dc, ch 2).*

Row 1 (right side): With tan, ch 243, dc in 4th ch from hook, dc in next 2 ch, * ch 2, sk 2 ch, dc in next 13 ch, (ch 2, sk 2 ch, dc in next ch) 3 times, ch 2, sk 2 ch, dc in next 13 ch, ch 2, sk 2 ch, dc in next 7 ch, repeat from * 3 times, ch 2, sk 2 ch, dc in next 13 ch, (ch 2, sk 2 ch, dc in next ch) 3 times, ch 2, sk 2 ch, dc in next 13 ch, ch 2, sk 2 ch, dc in next 4 ch, turn.
Row 2: Ch 5, sk 2 dc, dc in next dc, * 2 dc in next ch-2 sp, dc in next 10 dc, ch 2, sk 2 dc, dc in next dc, (ch 2, sk ch-2 sp, dc in next dc) 4 times, ch 2, sk 2 dc, dc in next 10 dc, 2 dc in next ch-2 sp, dc in next dc, (ch 2, sk 2 dc, dc in next dc) 2 times, repeat from * 3 times, 2 dc in next ch-2 sp, dc in next 10 dc, ch 2, sk 2 dc, dc in next dc, (ch 2, sk ch-2 sp, dc in next dc) 4 times, ch 2, sk 2 dc, dc in next 10

dc, 2 dc in next ch-2 sp, dc in next dc, ch 2, sk 2 dc, dc in next dc, turn.
Following graph and with ch-3 at beginning of rows beginning with solid block and ch-5 at beginning of rows beginning with open block, repeat each pattern of 16 blocks 5 times across and rows 1-24 four times. Turn.

Border:
Rnd 1 (right side): Working across side, sc in 1st dc, * (ch 2, sk 2 sts, sc in next st) across to corner, ch 2, sk 2 sts, (sc, ch 2, sc) in end st; working across end, (ch 1, sk over edge of dc, sc in top of next dc) across to corner, ch 1, sk over last dc, (sc, ch 2, sc) in end ch, repeat from * once, ending with sc, ch 2, join with sl st in 1st sc to complete last corner. Do not turn.
Rnd 2: Ch 1, working around entire outer edge, sc in each sc, 2 sc in each ch-2 sp, sc in each ch-1 sp, and (sc, ch 2, sc) in each corner ch-2 sp, join, turn.

Continued on page 14

Lacy wheels are charming in your favorite pastel shade of fuzzy bulky-weight yarn. This soft and fluffy throw makes a beautiful addition to any room.

Lace Medallions

By
JOAN DROST

Skill Level
Easy

Size
48" x 60"

Materials
4-ply fuzzy worsted-weight yarn: 32 oz. pale green
Hook size K/10½ (6.50mm)

Gauge
Large motif is 6" in diameter; small motif is 3" in diameter

Instructions

Large Motif (make 80):
Rnd 1: Ch 4, join to form ring, ch 4, (dc in ring, ch 1) 5 times, join with sl st in 3rd ch of ch-4.
Rnd 2: Ch 3, dc in same st, 2 dc in ch-1 sp, (2 dc in next dc, 2 dc in ch-1 sp) around, join with sl st in top of ch-3. (24)
Rnd 3: Ch 6, (sk next dc, dc in next dc, ch 3) around, join with sl st in 3rd ch of ch-6. (12)
Rnd 4: (Sc, 3 dc, sc) in each ch-3 sp around, join with sl st in 1st sc, fasten off.

Small Motif (make 63):
Rnd 1: Ch 4, join to form ring, ch 1, 8 sc in ring, join with sl st in 1st sc. (8)
Rnd 2: (Ch 8, sl st in next st, ch 6, sl st in next st) 4 times, fasten off.

Assembly:
With length of yarn and yarn needle, sew large motifs together in 10 strips of 8 motifs each, sewing each pair together at the tips of 2 corresponding petals.
Sew strips together by joining 2 petals on side of each motif.
Sew small motifs between large motifs.❀

Reminiscent of floral gardens and lazy days at the seashore, this easy-care afghan features lacy panels and delicate scallops in beige and three shades of lavender.

Scallops and Shells

By
LUCIA KARGE

Skill Level
Easy

Size
49" x 64"

Materials
2-ply chunky yarn: 36 oz. beige, 9 oz. dark purple, 6 oz. plum, 3 oz. lavender
Crochet hook size I/9 (5.50mm)

Gauge
3 dc = 1"; 5 dc rows = 3"

Instructions

Beige Lace Panels (make 3):
Row 1 (right side): With beige, ch 40, dc in 4th ch from hook, dc in each of next 3 ch, (sk 2 ch, 5 dc in next ch, ch 2, sk 3 ch, dc in each of next 5 ch) 3 times, turn.
Rows 2-105: Ch 3, dc in each of next 4 dc, (sk 2 ch, 5 dc in 1st dc of 5-dc group, ch 2, sk remaining 4 dc of group, dc in each of next 5 dc) 3 times, turn.
At end of row 105, fasten off.

Center Panel Trim:
First Edge:
Row 1: With right side up, join dk. purple in side edge of panel in row 1. Ch 1, work 157 hdc evenly spaced along edge, turn. (157)
Row 2: Ch 3, 2 dc in same st, sk 2 sts, sc in next st, (sk 2 sts, 5 dc in next st, sk 2 sts, sc in next st) across to within last 3 sts, sk 2 sts, 3 dc in last st, fasten off, turn.
Row 3: Join plum in 1st dc, ch 1, sc in same dc, 5 dc in next sc, (sc in 3rd dc of

5-dc group, 5 dc in next sc) across, ending with sc in 3rd dc of 3-dc group, fasten off, turn.
Row 4: Join dk. purple in 1st sc, ch 3, 2 dc in same sc, sc in 3rd dc of next 5-dc group, (5 dc in next sc, sc in 3rd dc of next 5-dc group) across, ending with 3 dc in last sc, fasten off, turn.
Rows 5-6: Repeat rows 3-4.
Row 7: Repeat row 3.
Row 8: Join lavender, ch 1, sc in same st, sc in each of next 5 dc, * yo, insert hook in next sc, draw up a lp, (yo, insert hook in same sc, draw up a lp) 3 times, yo, draw through all lps on hook, ch 1, sc in each of next 5 dc, repeat from * across, ending with sc in last sc, fasten off, turn.
Row 9: Join dk. purple, ch 1, hdc in each st across, fasten off.

Second Edge:
Row 1: With right side up, join dk. purple in second edge of same panel in row 105,

Continued on page 14

Scallops & Shells

Continued from page 12

ch 1, work 157 hdc evenly spaced along edge, turn. (157)

Rows 2-9: Repeat rows 2-9 of first edge. Center panel is complete.

Right Panel Trim:
Note: When completed, this panel is attached to the right of center panel.
Row 1: With right side up, join dk. purple in left edge of row 105, ch 1, work 157 hdc evenly spaced across edge, turn.
Row 2 (joining row): Holding center panel and right panel right sides together and working through both thicknesses, ch 1, sc in each hdc across, fasten off.

Right panel is complete.

Left Panel Trim:
Note: When completed, this panel is attached to the left of center panel.
Row 1: With right side up, join dk. purple in right edge of row 1, ch 1, work 157 hdc evenly spaced along edge, turn.
Row 2: Repeat row 2 of Right Panel Trim.

Top and Bottom Trim:
With right side up, join dk. purple in corner, ch 1, hdc in each st evenly across, fasten off.❖

Double Wedding Ring

Continued from page 8

Rnd 3: Ch 1, sc in each sc around, with (sc, ch 2, sc) in each corner, join, fasten off, turn.
Rnd 4: With off-white, draw up a lp in 2nd sc on end to the right of corner ch-2 sp on side, ch 1, sc in 1st sc, ch 1, sk 1 sc, (sc ch 2, sc) in corner ch-2 sp, * working across side, (ch 2, sk 2 ch, sc in next sc) across to corner, ch 2, sk 2 sc, (sc, ch 2, sc) in corner ch-2 sp; working across end, (ch 1, sk 1 sc, sc in next sc) across to corner, ch 1, sk 1 sc, (sc, ch 2, sc) in corner sp, repeat from * once, join last ch-1 with sl st in 1st sc, fasten off. Do not turn.
Rnd 5: Join lt. coral in any sc on edge, ch 3, dc in each sc and in each ch-1 sp around, working 2 dc in each ch-2 sp and (2 dc, ch 2, 2 dc) in each corner, join with sl st in top of ch 3, fasten off, turn.
Rnd 6: Join off-white in 2nd dc on end to the right of corner ch-2 sp on either side, ch 1, repeat rnd 4 working in dc sts instead of sc sts, join, fasten off, turn.
Rnd 7: Join tan in 4th sc on end to the right of corner ch-2 sp on either side, ch 3, repeat rnd 5, join. Do not turn.
Rnd 8: Ch 1, sc in 1st dc, sk 2 dc, (2 dc, ch 2, 2 dc) in next dc (shell made), sk 2 dc, sc in next dc, sk 2 dc, (3 dc, ch 2, 3 dc) in corner (corner shell made), * sk 2 dc, sc in next dc, sk 2 dc, shell in next dc, repeat from * around working corner shell in each corner, join with sl st in 1st sc. Do not turn.
Rnd 9: Sl st in next ch-2 sp, ch 3, 6 dc in same sp, ch 1, working around corner, sc in 2nd dc of corner shell, 9 dc in corner sp, sk 1 dc, sc in next dc, ch 1, * 7 dc in next ch-2 sp, ch 1, repeat from * around, working corner pattern in remaining corners; end with ch 1, join with sl st in top of ch-3. Do not turn.
Rnd 10: Sl st to center dc of next 7-dc group, ch 1, (sc, ch 3, sc) in same st, working around corner, ch 2, (sc, ch 3, sc) in next ch-1 sp, ch 2, sk sc and 1 dc, (sc, ch 3, sc) in next dc, ch 2, sk 2 dc, (sc, ch 3) 3 times in next dc, sc in same dc (center), ch 2, sk 2 dc, (sc, ch 3, sc) in next dc, ch 2, sk next dc and sc, (sc, ch 3, sc) in next ch-1 sp, * ch 2, sc, ch 3, sc in center dc of next 7-dc group, ch 2, sc in next ch-1 sp, repeat from * around, working corner pattern in remaining corners; end with ch 2, join with sl st in 1st sc, fasten off.

Finishing:

Leaving yarn attached to skein, thread lt. coral into yarn needle, working on sts of rnd 5 of border, easing yarn along as work progresses, weave a single strand under and over dcs, secure ends and fasten off.

Working on sts of rnd 3 of border, weave a double strand of lt. coral under and over scs as above, secure ends and fasten off.✿

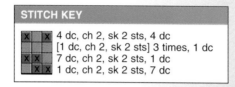

STITCH KEY

X	X	4 dc, ch 2, sk 2 sts, 4 dc
		[1 dc, ch 2, sk 2 sts] 3 times, 1 dc
X X		7 dc, ch 2, sk 2 sts, 1 dc
	X X	1 dc, ch 2, sk 2 sts, 7 dc

DOUBLE WEDDING RING

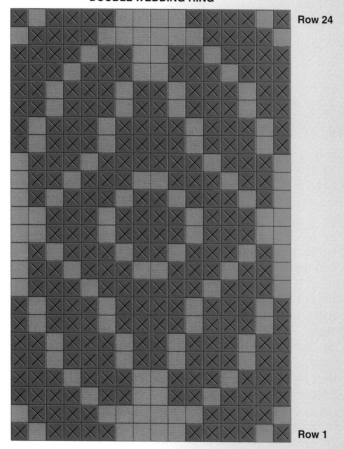

Row 24

Row 1

Delicate blossoms grace lacy, elegant panels in this beautiful afghan. It's a stunning romantic touch for a bedroom, draped across a bed, chair or chaise.

Victorian Lace

By
MELANIE MACDUFFIE

Skill Level
Average

Size
49" x 64"

Materials
4-ply worsted-weight yarn: 14 oz. dark green,
10½ each medium green and light green,
7 oz. each burgundy and rose, 3½ oz. pink
Hook size K/10½ (6.50mm)

Gauge
Flower is 3¾" across

Instructions

Flower Strips (make one with pink flowers and two each with rose and burgundy flowers):
Rnd 1: With flower color, ch 5, sl st in 1st ch to form ring, ch 1, 12 sc in ring, join with sl st in 1st sc.
Rnd 2: (Ch 3, sk 1 sc, sl st in next sc) 6 times.
Rnd 3: Ch 1, (sc, hdc, dc, hdc, sc) in each ch lp around, join with sl st in 1st sc.
Rnd 4: (Ch 3, sl st in 1st sc of next petal) around; join. Flip chains behind petals.
Rnd 5: Ch 1, (sc, hdc, dc, 2 tr, dc, hdc, sc) in each of 1st 3 ch lps, ch 15, sl st in 5th ch from hook to form new ring for next flower.
Beginning with ch 1, 12 sc in ring, repeat rnds 1-5 11 times, omitting ch 15 after final flower.

Finishing:
Rnd 1: * Continue around flower, working 3 more petals as in rnd 5 **, sk 1st 5 ch of connecting ch between flowers, sc in next 5 ch, repeat from * 10 times, repeat from * to **, join with sl st in next sc, end off.

Green Lace:
Rnd 1: Sk 1 st, join lt. green in next st, * (ch 5, sk 2 sts, sc in next st, ch 5, sk 4 sts, sc in next st) 2 times, ch 5, sk 2 sts, sc in next st, ch 1, dc in 3rd st of connecting section, ch 1, sc in 1st dc of 1st petal of next flower, repeat from * 10 times, (ch 5, sk 2 sts, sc in next st, ch 5, sk 4 sts, sc in next st) 3 times **, repeat from * to **, ending with sl st in beginning st.
Rnd 2: Sl st in next 2 ch, sc in lp, ch 5, sc in next lp, ** ch 7, dc in same lp, (ch 5, sc in next lp) 2 times, ch 5, dc in next lp, * ch 3, dc in next ch-5 lp, (ch 5, sc in next lp) 3 times, ch 5, dc in next lp, repeat from * 9 times, ch 3, dc in next ch-5 lp, (ch 5, sc in next lp) 2 times, ch 5, dc in next lp, ch 7,

Continued on page 22

Realistically shaded floral blocks are set against a background of rich rose in this stunning heirloom creation. An old-fashioned white ruffle adds the finishing touch.

Floral Tapestry

By
GLENDA WINKLEMAN

Skill Level
Easy

Size
45" x 75"

Materials
4-ply worsted-weight yarn: 40 oz. white,
30 oz. medium pink, 12 oz. light pink, 1 oz. each yellow,
silver, dark green, green, medium blue and light blue
Afghan crochet hook size J/10 (6.00mm),
crochet hook size H/8 (5.00mm), yarn needle

Gauge
Afghan st: 5 sts = 1"; 4 rows = 1"
Groups of 3 dc: 2 groups = 1½"; 3 rows = 1½"

Instructions

Afghan Stitch Blocks (make 8):
Rows 1-47: With afghan hook and white, ch 50, work afghan st for a total of 47 rows, fasten off.
Border Trim:
Rnd 1: With crochet hook, join med. pink in top right corner, ch 3, * dc in each st across to corner, (dc, ch 2, dc) in corner, dc in end of each row down side, (dc, ch 2, dc) in corner, repeat from * around, ending with dc in last corner, ch 2, sl st in top of ch-3, fasten off.
Note: When working rnd 2, sometimes when reaching corners, you will have one too many or one too few stitches. When this happens, instead of skipping 2 sts, you may skip 1 or skip 3 to maintain 17 groups of 3 dc on each side of square.
Rnd 2: Join pink in corner ch-2 sp, ch 3, 2 dc in same sp, * (sk 2 sts, 3 dc in next st) across to corner, (3 dc, ch 2, 3 dc) in corner sp, repeat from * around, ending with 3 dc in corner sp, ch 2, sl st in top of ch-3, fasten off.

Cross Stitch:
Follow chart to cross stitch design on each block.

Double Crochet Blocks (make 7):
Row 1: With crochet hook and med. pink, ch 49, 2 dc in 4th ch from hook, (sk 2 ch, 3 dc in next ch) across, turn. (16 dc groups)
Row 2: Ch 3, (3 dc in sp after next dc group) across, ch 3, sl st in last dc, sl st in each ch just made. (15 dc groups)
Row 3: Ch 3, 2 dc in ch-3 sp, (3 dc in sp after next dc group) across, ending with 3 dc in ch-3 sp, turn.
Rows 4-31: Repeat rows 2-3. At end of row 31, fasten off.

Continued on page 23

Celebrate the holidays in Victorian style with a magnificent afghan. Featuring vibrant pinks and reds accented with forest green, each block makes a great carry-along project.

Holiday Blossoms

By
KATHERINE ENG

Skill Level
Average

Size
42" x 59"

Materials
4-ply knitting worsted-weight yarn: 14 oz. each bright pink and forest green, 10½ oz. each dark pink and red
Crochet hook size F/5 (4.00mm)

Gauge
Rnds 1 and 2 = 2" across; block = 5½" square

Instructions

Block (make 70):
Rnd 1: With brt. pink, ch 4, join with sl st to form ring, ch 1, 8 sc in ring, join with sl st in 1st sc. (8)
Rnd 2: Ch 3, (retaining last lp of each dc on hook, work 3 dc in sc, yo, draw through all lps on hook, ch 2) 8 times, join with sl st in top of 1st cluster, fasten off. (8 clusters)
Rnd 3: Join forest green in any ch-2 sp, ch 1, 4 sc in each ch-2 sp around, join.
Rnd 4: Ch 1, sc in 1st 3 sc, hdc in next sc, (2 dc, ch 2, 2 dc) in next sc, * hdc in next sc, sc in next 5 sc, hdc in next sc, (2 dc, ch 2, 2 dc) in next sc, repeat from * around, ending with hdc in next sc, sc in last 2 sc, join, fasten off.
Rnd 5: Join dk. pink in 3rd st (hdc) to the left of any corner ch-2 sp, ch 1, sc in same st as beg ch-1, * sk 2 sts, (2 dc, ch 2, 2 dc) in next st, sk 2 sts, sc in next st, sk 2 sts, (3 dc, ch 2, 3 dc) in corner sp, sk 2 sts, sc in next st, repeat from * around, join with sl st in 1st sc, fasten off.

Rnd 6: Join red in any ch-2 sp at center between corners, ch 1, * sc in ch-2 sp, sc in next dc, hdc in next dc, dc in next sc, hdc in next dc, dc in next 2 dc, (2 dc, ch 2, 2 dc) in corner sp, dc in next 2 dc, hdc in next dc, dc in next sc, hdc in next dc, sc in next dc, repeat from * around, join with sl st in 1st sc, fasten off.
Rnd 7: Join brt. pink in 2nd dc to the left of any corner sp, ch 1, sc in 1st dc, (ch 1, sk 1 st, sc in next st) around, with (ch 1, sk 1 st, ch 3, sc) in each corner sp, join with sl st in 1st sc, fasten off.

Assembly:
With yarn needle and brt. pink, holding blocks right sides together and working in back lps only, whipstitch blocks together in strips of 7; whipstitch strips together.

Border:
Rnd 1 (right side): Join brt. pink in any sc on edge, ch 1, sc in each sc, ch-1 sp
Continued on next page

Holiday Blossoms

Continued from page 21

and ch-3 sp of block, working hdc in each seam and (sc, ch 3, sc) in each corner of afghan, join with sl st in 1st sc.

Rnd 2: Ch 1, sc in each st around, with (sc, ch 3, sc) in each corner, join with sl st in 1st sc, turn.

Rnd 3: Ch 1, sc in next sc, (ch 1, sk 1 sc, sc in next sc) around, with (ch 1, sk 1 sc, sc, ch 3, sc) in each corner, join with sl st in 1st sc, fasten off, turn.

Rnd 4: Join forest green in any ch-1 sp on edge, ch 3, dc in each sc and each ch-1 sp around, working (2 dc, ch 2, 2 dc) in each corner sp, join with sl st in top of ch-3, turn.

Rnd 5: Ch 1, sc in next dc, (ch 1, sk 1 dc, sc in next dc) around, with (sc, ch 2, sc) in each corner sp; sc in last sc, join with sl st in 1st sc, turn.

Rnd 6: Ch 3, dc in each sc and in each ch-1 sp around, with (2 dc, ch 2, 2 dc) in each corner sp, join with sl st in top of ch-3, fasten off, turn.

Rnd 7: Join dk. pink in 12th dc to the left of any corner sp, ch 1, sc in 1st dc, (ch 2, sk 2 dc, sc in next dc) around, with (ch 2, sk 2 dc, sc, ch 3, sc) in each corner sp; end with ch 2, join with sl st in 1st sc, turn.

Rnd 8: Sl st in next ch-2 sp, ch 3, 2 dc in same sp, (ch 1, 3 dc in next ch-2 sp) around, with (ch 1, 3 dc, ch 2, 3 dc) in each corner; end with ch 1, join with sl st in top of ch-3, fasten off, turn.

Rnd 9: Join red in any ch-1 sp, ch 1, sc in same sp, (ch 2, sc in next ch-1 sp) around, with (ch 2, sc, ch 3, sc) in each corner; end with ch 2, join with sl st in 1st sc, turn.

Rnd 10: Sl st in next ch-2 sp, ch 1, sc in same sp, (ch 3, sc in next ch-2 sp) around, with (ch 3, sc , ch 3, sc) in each corner; end with ch 3, join with sl st in 1st sc, fasten off.❈

Victorian Lace

Continued from page 16

dc in same lp, (ch 5, sc in next lp) 4 times, repeat from **, ending with sl st in beginning sc, fasten off.

Rnd 3: Join med. green in previous corner lp, ** (ch 5, sc in next lp) 5 times, * (ch 5, sc in next lp) 2 times, ch 5, dc in next lp, ch 5, sk ch-3 lp, dc in next lp, repeat from * 10 times, (ch 5, sc in next lp) 3 times, repeat from **, ending with sl st in beginning st.

Rnd 4: Sl st in next 2 ch, sc in lp, (ch 5, sc in next lp) around, ending with sl st in beginning sc, end off.

Rnd 5: Join dk. green in any corner lp, * ch 7, sc in same lp, (ch 5, sc in next lp) to next corner lp, repeat from * 3 times, ending with sl st in beginning st.

Repeat rnds 1-5 of lace for each panel.

Rnd 6 (for 1st burgundy panel only):
Continuing with dk. green, join in any corner lp, * ch 7, sc in same lp, (ch 5, sc in next lp) to next corner lp * **, repeat from * to * 3 times, join in beginning sc.

Joining panels:

Rnd 6 (for 1st rose panel): Work as for rnd 6 above through **, repeat from * to * once, lay long unworked edge next to either edge of burgundy panel (1st panel), ch 3, sl st in dk. green corner lp of 1st panel, ch 4, sc in same corner lp of rose panel (2nd panel), (ch 3, sl st in next lp of 1st panel, ch 2, sc in next lp of 2nd panel) to corner lp of 2nd panel, ch 4, sl st in corner lp of 1st panel, ch 3, sc in same corner lp of 2nd panel as before, (ch 5, sc in next lp) to corner, ending, join with sl st in 1st sc.

Work rnd 6 as above for remaining panels, connecting panels in order as shown in photo.

Border:

Rnd 1: Join dk. green in any corner, * (sc, hdc, 5 dc, hdc, dc) in corner lp, (sc, hdc, dc, hdc, sc) in each lp to next corner,

repeat from * around, sl st in 1st sc.
Rnd 2: Sl st in hdc, sc in dc, * ch 7, sk 3 dc, sc in next dc, (ch 5, sk 4 sts, sc in dc) to next corner cluster, repeat from * around, sl st in 1st sc.

Rnd 3: Sl st in next 2 ch, sc in lp, * ch 7, sc in same lp, (ch 5, sc in next lp) to next corner, repeat from * around, sl st in 1st sc.
Rnd 4: Repeat rnd 1, fasten off.❀

Floral Tapestry
Continued from page 18

Border Trim:
Rnd 1: With crochet hook, join lt. pink in corner, ch 3, 2 dc between 1st and 2nd st of dc group, 3 dc in each sp between dc groups across to corner, (3 dc, ch 2, 3 dc) between 2nd and 3rd st of last dc group before corner, (3 dc in next ch-3 sp) down side, (3 dc, ch 2, 3 dc) in bottom of corner dc, 3 dc in each sp between dc groups across, (3 dc, ch 2, 3 dc) between 2nd and 3rd st of last dc group before corner, 3 dc in each ch-3 sp down side, end with 3 dc in beginning st, ch 2, sl st in top of ch-3. (17 dc groups each side)

Assembly:
Following chart, sew blocks together.

Border:
Rnd 1: With crochet hook, attach white in corner ch-2 sp, (ch 3, 6 dc) in same sp, sc in next sp between dc groups, (7 dc in next sp between dc groups, sc in next sp between dc groups) around, counting each seam line as a sp between dc groups; join with sl st in top of ch-3, do not turn.
Rnd 2: Ch 3, dc in same st, (2 dc in each dc, sc in each sc) around, join with sl st in top of ch-3.
Rnd 3: Ch 3, dc in next dc, (dc in each dc, sl st in each sc) around, join with sl st in top of ch-3, fasten off.❀

COLOR KEY	
☒	Med. pink
■	Dk. green
◩	Green
■	Silver
Ⅰ	Pink
▽	Yellow
◪	Lt. blue
■	Med. blue

FLORAL TAPESTRY

Flower	Cluster	Flower
Cluster	Flower	Cluster
Flower	Cluster	Flower
Cluster	Flower	Cluster
Flower	Cluster	Flower

*Bring a little love into your country-style home with this cozy, cuddly warmer.
Pretty hearts are easy to make in a dimensional long double crochet stitch.*

Country Hearts

By
BONNIE FRIDLEY

Skill Level
Easy

Size
46" x 68"

Materials
4-ply worsted-weight yarn: 42 oz. country blue, 35 oz. white
Hook size N/15 (10mm)

Gauge
3 sc = 1"; 3 sc rows = 1"

Instructions

Notes:
1. Ldc (long double crochet): Yo, insert hook around post of sc 2 rows below, draw up a lp even with work, (yo, draw through 2 lps on hook) 2 times.
2. Fldc (front long double crochet): Yo, insert hook around long dc 2 rows below to the left, draw up a lp even with work, (yo, draw through 2 lps on hook) 2 times.
3. Bldc (back long double crochet): Yo, insert hook around long dc 2 rows below to the right, draw up a lp even with work, (yo, draw through 2 lps on hook) 2 times.
4. Vldc (V long double crochet): Yo, insert hook around long dc two rows below to the right, draw up a lp even with work, yo, insert hook around long dc two rows below to the left, draw up a lp even with work, yo, draw through 4 lps on hook, yo, draw through 2 lps on hook.

Panel #1 (make 4):
Row 1: With country blue, ch 14, sc in 2nd ch from hook and in each ch across, turn. (13)

Row 2: Ch 1, sc in each sc across, turn.
Row 3: Ch 1, sc in next 6 sc, long dc, sc in next 6 sc, turn.
Rows 4, 6, 8, 10 and 12: Repeat row 2.
Row 5: Ch 1, sc in next 4 sc, fldc, sc in next 3 sc, bldc, sc in next 4 sc, turn.
Row 7: Ch 1, sc in next 3 sc, fldc, sc in next 5 sc, bldc, sc in next 3 sc, turn.
Row 9: Ch 1, sc in next 2 sc, fldc, sc in next 7 sc, bldc, sc in next 2 sc, turn.
Row 11: Ch 1, sc in next 2 sc, fldc, sc in next 3 sc, ldc, sc in next 3 sc, bldc, sc in next 2 sc, turn.
Row 13: Ch 1, sc in next 3 sc, Vldc, sc in next 5 sc, Vldc, sc in next 3 sc, turn.
Rows 14-15: Repeat row 2.
Repeat rows 2-15 12 more times. Fasten off.

Panel #2 (make 2):
Row 1: With white, ch 26, sc in 2nd ch from hook and in each ch across, turn. (25)
Row 2: Ch 1, sc in each sc across, turn.

Continued on page 26

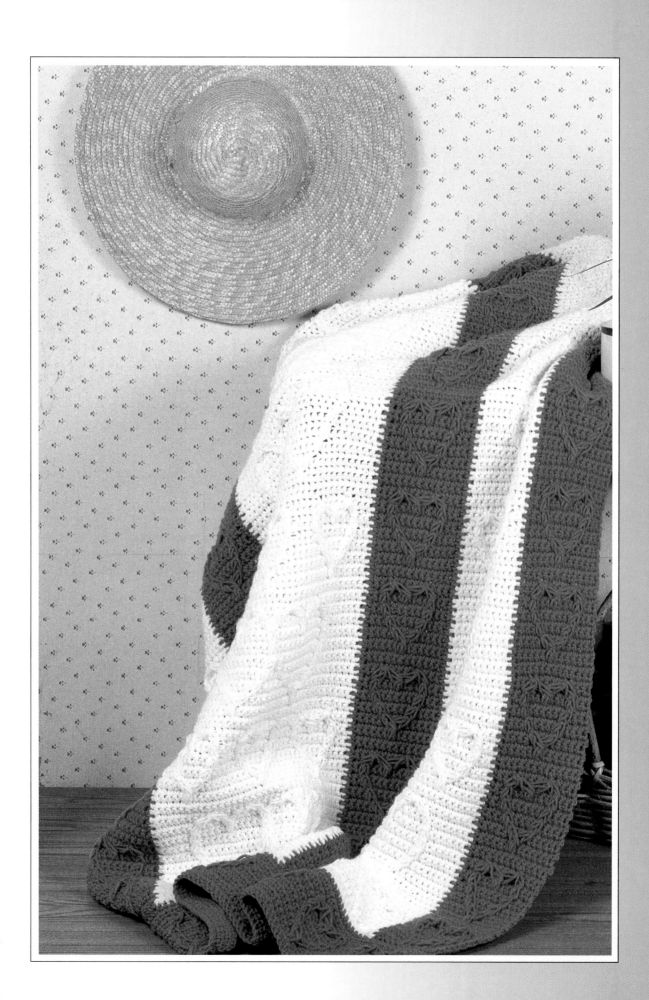

Country Hearts

Continued from page 24

Row 3: Ch 1, sc in next 6 sc, ldc, sc in next 11 sc, ldc, sc in next 6 sc, turn.
Row 4 and all even-numbered rows: Repeat row 2.
Row 5: Ch 1, sc in next 4 sc, fldc, sc in next 3 sc, bldc, sc in next 7 sc, fldc, sc in next 3 sc, bldc, sc in next 4 sc, turn.
Row 7: Ch 1, sc in next 3 sc, fldc, sc in next 5 sc, bldc, sc in next 5 sc, fldc, sc in next 5 sc, bldc, sc in next 3 sc, turn.
Row 9: Ch 1, sc in next 2 sc, fldc, sc in next 7 sc, bldc, sc in next 3 sc, fldc, sc in next 7 sc, bldc, sc in next 2 sc, turn.
Row 11: Ch 1, sc in next 2 sc, fldc, sc in next 3 sc, ldc, sc in next 3 sc, bldc, sc in next 3 sc, fldc, sc in next 3 sc, ldc, sc in next 3 sc, bldc, sc in next 2 sc, turn.
Row 13: Ch 1, sc in next 3 sc, (Vldc, sc in next 5 sc) 3 times, Vldc, sc in next 3 sc, turn.
Row 15: Repeat row 2.
Row 17: Ch 1, sc in next 12 sc, ldc, sc in next 12 sc, turn.
Row 19: Ch 1, sc in next 10 sc, fldc, sc in next 3 sc, bldc, sc in next 10 sc, turn.
Row 21: Ch 1, sc in next 8 sc, fldc, sc in next 7 sc, bldc, sc in next 8 sc, turn.
Row 23: Ch 1, sc in next 7 sc, fldc, sc in next 9 sc, bldc, sc in next 7 sc, turn.
Row 25: Ch 1, sc in next 6 sc, fldc, sc in next 11 sc, bldc, sc in next 6 sc, turn.
Row 27: Ch 1, sc in next 6 sc, ldc, sc in next 11 sc, ldc, sc in next 6 sc, turn.
Row 29: Ch 1, sc in next 6 sc, ldc, sc in next 5 sc, ldc, sc in next 5 sc, ldc, sc in next 6 sc, turn.
Row 31: Ch 1, sc in next 7 sc, bldc, sc in next 3 sc, fldc, sc in next sc, bldc, sc in next 3 sc, fldc, sc in next 7 sc, turn.
Row 33: Ch 1, sc in next 9 sc, Vldc, sc in next 5 sc, Vldc, sc in next 9 sc, turn.
Row 35: Repeat row 2.
Repeat rows 2-35 4 more times, ending with row 33 on last repeat. Fasten off.

Panel #3 (make 1):
Row 1: With white, ch 38, sc in 2nd ch from hook and in each ch across, turn. (37)
Row 2: Ch 1, sc in each sc across, turn.

Row 3: Ch 1, sc in next 6 sc, ldc, sc in next 11 sc, ldc, sc in next 11 sc, ldc, sc in next 6 sc, turn.
Row 4 and all even-numbered rows: Repeat row 2.
Row 5: Ch 1, sc in next 4 sc, fldc, sc in next 3 dc, bldc, dc in next 7 sc, fldc, sc in next 3 sc, bldc, sc in next 7 sc, fldc, sc in next 3 sc, bldc, sc in next 4 sc, turn.
Row 7: Ch 1, sc in next 3 sc, fldc, sc in next 5 sc, bldc, sc in next 5 sc, fldc, sc in next 5 sc, bldc, sc in next 5 sc, fldc, sc in next 5 sc, bldc, sc in next 3 sc, turn.
Row 9: Ch 1, sc in next 2 sc, fldc, sc in next 7 sc, bldc, sc in next 3 sc, fldc, sc in next 7 sc, bldc, sc in next 3 sc, fldc, sc in next 7 sc, bldc, sc in next 2 sc, turn.
Row 11: Ch 1, sc in next 2 sc, (ldc, sc in next 3 sc) 8 times, ldc, sc in next 2 sc, turn.
Row 13: Ch 1, sc in next 3 sc, (Vldc, sc in next 5 sc) 5 times, Vldc, sc in next 3 sc, turn.
Row 15: Repeat row 2.
Row 17: Ch 1, sc in next 12 sc, ldc, sc in next 11 dc, ldc, sc in next 12 dc, turn.
Row 19: Ch 1, sc in next 10 sc, fldc, sc in next 3 sc, bldc, sc in next 7 sc, fldc, sc in next 3 sc, bldc, sc in next 10 sc, turn.
Row 21: Ch 1, sc in next 8 sc, fldc, sc in next 7 sc, bldc, sc in next 3 sc, fldc, sc in next 7 sc, bldc, sc in next 8 sc, turn.
Row 23: Ch 1, sc in next 7 sc, fldc, sc in next 9 sc, bldc, sc in next sc, fldc, sc in next 9 sc, bldc, sc in next 7 sc, turn.
Row 25: Ch 1, sc in next 6 sc, fldc, sc in next 11 sc, Vldc, sc in next 11 sc, bldc, sc in next 6 sc, turn.
Row 27: Ch 1, sc in next 6 sc, ldc, sc in next 11 sc, ldc, sc in next 11 sc, ldc, sc in next 6 sc, turn.
Row 29: Ch 1, sc in next 6 sc, (ldc, sc in next 5 sc) 4 times, ldc, sc in next 6 sc, turn.
Row 31: Ch 1, sc in next 7 sc, bldc, sc in next 3 sc, fldc, sc in next sc, bldc, sc in next 3 sc, fldc, sc in next sc, bldc, sc in next 3 sc, fldc, sc in next sc, bldc, sc in next 3 sc, fldc, sc in next 7 sc, turn.
Row 33: Ch 1, sc in next 9 sc, Vldc, sc in

next 5 sc, Vldc, sc in next 5 sc, Vldc, sc in next 9 sc, turn.
Row 35: Repeat row 2.
Repeat rows 2-35 4 times, ending with row 33 on last repeat. Fasten off.

Panel #4 (make 2):
Row 1: With country blue, ch 134, sc in 2nd ch from hook and in each ch across, turn. (133)
Row 2: Ch 1, sc in each sc across, turn.
Rows 3, 5, 7, 9, 11, 13, 15: Repeat row 2.
Row 4: Ch 1, sc in next 6 sc, (ldc, sc in next 11 sc) 10 times, ldc, sc in next 6 sc, turn.
Row 6: Ch 1, sc in next 3 sc, (fldc, sc in next 3 sc, bldc, sc in next 7 sc) 10 times, fldc, sc in next 5 sc, bldc, sc in next 3 sc, turn.
Row 8: Ch 1, sc in next 3 sc, (fldc, sc in next 5 sc, bldc, sc in next 5 sc) 10 times, fldc, sc in next 5 sc, bldc, sc in next 3 sc, turn.
Row 10: Ch 1, sc in next 2 sc, (fldc, sc in next 7 sc, bldc, sc in next 3 sc) 10 times, fldc, sc in next 7 sc, bldc, sc in next 2 sc, turn.
Row 12: Ch 1, sc in next 2 sc, (ldc, sc in next 3 sc) 32 times, ldc, sc in next 2 sc, turn.
Row 14: Ch 1, sc in next 3 sc, (Vldc, sc in next 5 sc) 21 times, Vldc, sc in next 3 sc, turn.
Row 16: Ch 1, sc in each sc across, fasten off.

Finishing:
To join panels, following panel placement diagram, holding right sides together and working through both thicknesses, join country blue with sl st, ch 1, sc evenly spaced across. Repeat until all panels are joined.❂

COUNTRY HEARTS

Panel Placement

Comforts of Home

The most beautiful home is one that is filled with touches that delight the owner and visitor alike. Favorite things collected over the years can be displayed in perfect harmony with new additions like a tulip-patterned folk afghan or a quilt-like blanket made in many different colors. Snuggle up with one of these lovely afghans, a cup of tea and a good book, and enjoy your home sweet home.

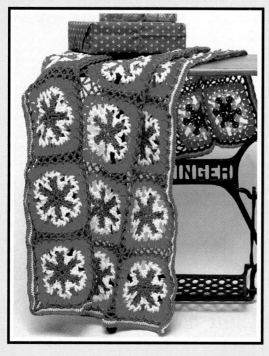

Folk Art Tulips

By
URSULA MICHAEL

Skill Level
Average

Size
50" x 62"

Materials
4-ply worsted-weight yarn: 31½ oz. eggshell, 17½ oz. red
Hook size J/10 (6.00mm), yarn needle

Gauge
12 sc = 3"; 12 rows = 3"

Instructions

Notes: Folk art designs are cross stitched after panels are completed. Work all sc sts in front lps only to create the grid for cross stitching.

Panel A (make 2):
With red, ch 240.
Rows 1-6: Ch 1, sc in each st across, turn.
Rows 7-24: With eggshell, ch 1, sc in each st across, turn.
At end of row 24, fasten off.

Panel B (make 2):
With red, ch 240.
Rows 1-6: Ch 1, sc in each st across, turn.
Rows 7-20: With eggshell, ch 1, sc in each st across, turn.
Rows 21-23: With red, ch 1, sc in each st across, turn.
At end of row 23, fasten off.

Panel C (make 1):
With eggshell, ch 240.
Rows 1-79: Ch 1, sc in each st across, turn.

At end of row 79, fasten off.

Cross Stitch:
Work all cross stitch with red. One sc equals one block on graph. Using tapestry needle and one strand of yarn, work one "X" on each sc as indicated by color blocks on graph. Repeat patterns along length of panels.

Assembly:
Holding right sides together, sew one panel B to each side of panel C; sew one panel A to each panel B.

Ruffle Edging:
Join eggshell to any corner; work along length.
Row 1: Ch 1, sc in each of 1st 3 sc, * sk 2 sts, 5 dc in next st, sk 2 sts, sc in next st, repeat from * across, ending with 3 sc, fasten off.
Row 2: Join red, ch 1, sc (in front lp only) in next 4 sc, 2 sc in top of shell, * sc in

Continued on page 32

Folk Art Tulips

Continued from page 30

each of next 2 sts, sk 1 st, sc in each of next 2 sts, 2 sc in next st, repeat from * across, ending with 1 sc in each st to end.

Width Trim:
With red, work 2 rows sc across top and bottom width.

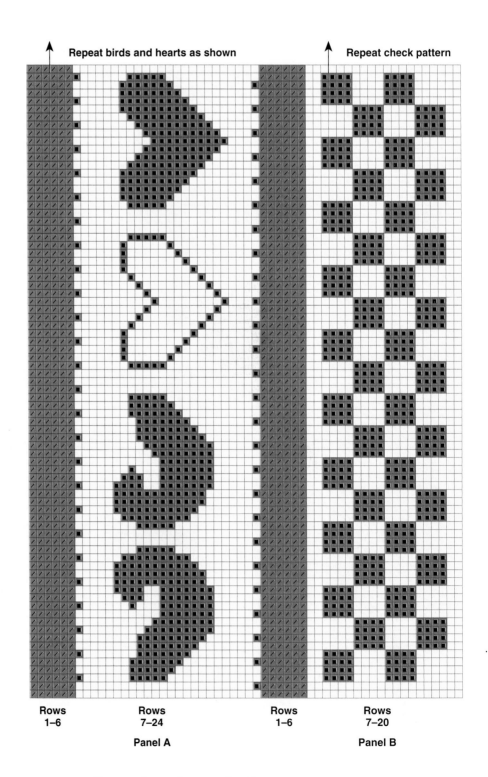

Repeat birds and hearts as shown

Repeat check pattern

COLOR KEY
Red MC chain
Red cross-stitch

Rows 1–6

Rows 7–24

Rows 1–6

Rows 7–20

Panel A

Panel B

Fringe:

For each fringe, cut six 12" strands of yarn; fold strands in half, draw fold through st at bottom of afghan, draw cut ends through fold, pull to secure. Attach fringe as shown in photo; trim ends.❀

FOLK ART TULIPS

Repeat flowers, alternating sizes A and B

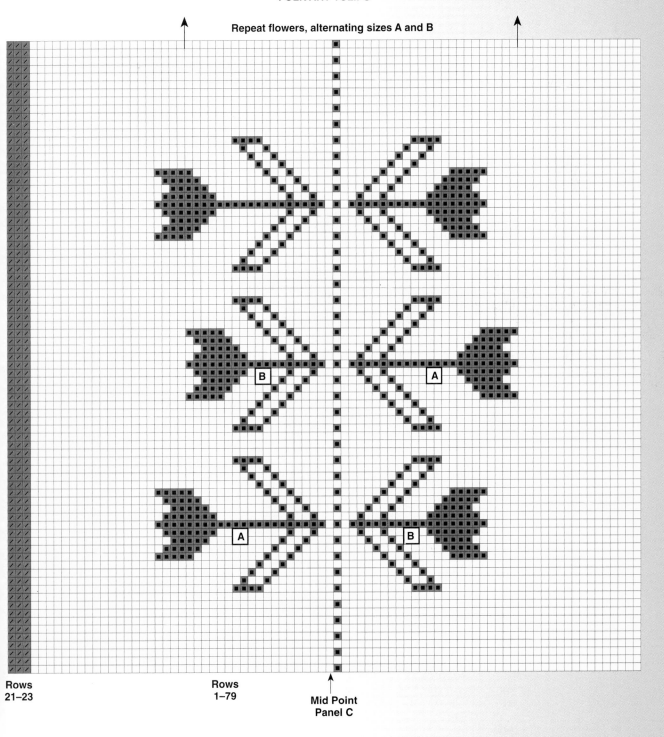

Rows 21–23

Rows 1–79

Mid Point Panel C

Use harmonious colors of leftover yarn to create an afghan that's just right for the feline-lover on your gift list. Perky bows can be tied with yarn or narrow satin ribbon.

Purrfectly Pretty

By
JUDITH STOVER

Skill Level
Easy

Size
42" x 49"; block = 9½" x 12"

Materials
4-ply worsted-weight yarn: 28 oz. off-white (MC), 1 oz. each 8 variegated or ombre colors (CC), 1 oz. each 8 solid colors (CC)
Hook size G/6 (4.50mm)

Gauge
7 sc = 2"; 7 sc rows = 2"

Instructions

Note: *When changing colors, work off last 2 lps of 1st color with 2nd color.*

Block (make 16):
Row 1: With off-white, ch 34, sc in 2nd ch from hook and in each ch across, turn. (33)
Row 2: Ch 1, sc in each sc across, turn.
Rows 3-41: Ch 1, following graph and changing colors as indicated, sc in each st across, turn.
At end of row 41, fasten off.

Assembly:
Holding right sides together, sew blocks together in 4 rows of 4 blocks.

Border:
Rnd 1: Join off-white with sc in any sc, sc evenly around outer edge with 3 sc in each corner, join with sl st in 1st sc.
Rnd 2: Ch 1, sc in each sc around with 3 sc in each center corner st, join with sl st in 1st sc.
Rnd 3: Ch 1, (sc in next 2 sc, ch 3, sk next sc) around, join with sl st in 1st sc, fasten off.

Finishing:
With a double strand of off-white, tie bows at neckline of each cat; trim ends evenly.❀

Graph on page 43

Warm up those crisp autumn evenings with a cozy blanket created in bronze, blue and green. Luxurious fringe and a rickrack edging complete the distinctive look.

Chevron Shells

By
KATHERINE ENG

Skill Level
Average

Size
39" x 53"

Materials
4-ply worsted-weight yarn: 24½ oz. bright blue,
10½ oz. bright green, 7 oz. rust, 3½ oz. country red
Hook size F/5 (4.00mm)

Gauge
2 shell patterns across = 2"; 3 shell rows = 1½"

Instructions

Row 1 (right side): With blue, ch 310, dc in 4th ch from hook, * sk 2 ch, sc in next ch, [sk 2 ch, (2 dc, ch 2, 2 dc) in next ch (shell made), sk 2 ch, sc in next ch] 2 times, sk 1 ch, shell in next ch, sk 1 ch, sc in next ch, (sk 2 ch, shell in next ch, sk 2 ch, sc in next ch) 2 times, sk 2 ch, 2 dc in next ch **, sk 4 ch, 2 dc in next ch *, repeat pattern from * to * 7 times, ending at ** on last repeat, turn, sl st in next sc, fasten off, turn.

Row 2: Join rust in 1st sc, ch 3, dc in same sc, * (sc in ch-2 sp of next shell, shell in next sc) 2 times, sk 1 dc, sc in next dc, shell in ch-2 sp, sc in next dc, (shell in next sc, sc in ch-2 sp of next shell) 2 times, 2 dc in next sc **, sk 4 dc, 2 dc in next sc, repeat from * to * across, ending at ** on last repeat, turn, sl st in next sc, fasten off.

Row 3: With green, repeat row 2.

Row 4: With blue, repeat row 2, do not fasten off.

Row 5: Continuing with blue, repeat row 2.

Row 6: With red, repeat row 2.
Continue pattern rows as follows: 1 green, 2 blue, 1 rust, 1 green and 4 blue.
Repeat with 1 rust, 1 red, 1 green, 2 blue, 1 rust, 1 green, 2 blue, 1 red, 1 green, 4 blue.
For last pattern repeat, begin with rust and work 1 final row of blue. At end of last blue row, ch 1, turn.

Border:
Across bottom end: Sc in end dc, ch 1, sk 1 dc, sc in next sc, *[ch 1, sk 2 dc, (sc, ch 2, sc) in ch-2 sp of next shell, ch 1, sk 2 dc, sc in next sc] 2 times, ch 2, sk 2 dc, (sc, ch 2, sc) in ch-2 sp at point, ch 2, sk 2 dc, sc in next sc **, [ch 1, sk 2 dc, (sc, ch 2, sc) in ch-2 sp of next shell, ch 1, sk 2 dc, sc in next sc] 2 times, ch 1, sk 4 dc, sc in next sc *, repeat from * to * across, ending at ** after last repeat on left side of point, ch 1, sk 1 dc, (sc, ch 2, sc) in top of end ch-3.

Continued on page 42

Luscious panels in two shades of coral are highlighted by diamonds and blocks, and finished with slim borders, pointed ends and decorative tassels.

Harlequin Tassels

By
DAISY WATSON

Skill Level
Average

Size
56" x 67"

Materials
4-ply worsted-weight yarn: 31 oz. coral, 26 oz. light coral
Hook size I/9 (5.50mm)

Gauge
6 dc = 2"; 2 dc rows = 1"

Instructions

Note: *Hdc cl st (hdc cluster st): Yo, insert hook in next st, draw up a lp, yo, insert hook in same st, draw up a lp, yo, draw through all 5 lps on hook, ch 1.*

Coral Panel (make 4):
Row 1: With coral, ch 4, dc in 4th ch from hook, turn. (2)
Row 2: Ch 3, dc in same st as beg ch-3, 2 dc in next dc, turn. (4)
Row 3: Ch 3, dc in same st as beg ch-3, dc in next 2 dc, 2 dc in next st, turn. (6)
Rows 4-11: Ch 3, dc in same st as beg ch-3, dc in each st across to last st, 2 dc in last st, turn. (22)
Rows 12-17: Ch 3, dc in each dc across, turn. (22)
Note: *Do not fasten off; work over yarn not in use.*
Row 18 (right side): Continuing with coral, ch 3, dc in next 9 sts; with lt. coral, hdc cl in next 2 sts, with coral, dc in next 10 sts, turn.
Row 19: With coral, ch 1, sc in each st and hdc cl across, turn. (22 sc)

Row 20: With coral, ch 3, dc in next 8 sts; with lt. coral, hdc cl in each of next 4 sts; with coral, dc in next 9 sts, turn.
Row 21: Repeat row 19.
Row 22: With coral, ch 3, dc in next 7 sts; with lt. coral, hdc cl in next 6 sts; with coral, dc in next 8 sts, turn.
Row 23: Repeat row 19.
Row 24: With coral, ch 3, dc in next 6 sts; with lt. coral, hdc cl in next 8 sts; with coral, dc in next 7 sts, turn.
Row 25: Repeat row 19.
Row 26: Repeat row 22.
Row 27: Repeat row 19.
Row 28: Repeat row 20.
Row 29: Repeat row 19.
Row 30: Repeat row 18; fasten off lt. coral; turn.
Row 31: Ch 3, dc in each dc and in top of each hdc cl across, turn. (22)
Rows 32-35: Ch 3, dc in each dc across, turn.
Row 36: With coral, dc in next 6 sts; with lt. coral, hdc cl in next 8 sts; with coral, dc

Continued on page 43

Nine colorful cottages create a charming country village on this generous-sized afghan. It's perfect for snuggling by the fire in the den or family room.

Country Cottages

By
LINDA HAMMONDS

Skill Level
Challenging

Size
68" x 75"

Materials
4-ply worsted-weight yarn: 28 oz. each off-white and rust,
24 oz. royal blue, 16 oz. medium blue
Hook sizes H/8 (5.00mm) and J/10 (6.00mm)

Gauge
With hook size J, 3 sc = 1"; 3 sc rows = 1"

Instructions

Notes:
1. House pattern starts at row 1 of graph on section 1. Last row of house pattern ends with last stitch of section 4.
2. Each block is worked in 8 sections in order indicated on graph.
3. Each section is joined to previous section as work progresses, with a sl st in corresponding row of previous section. When a row is completed, sl st to corresponding row on previous section, ch 1, and turn to start following row. OR, if desired, sections may be completed separately and sewn together.
4. Design as shown on graph is right side. The dot within a square on graph is the point at which a section is begun. For example, for section 2, begin on wrong side in next st beyond section 1.
5. Each block on graph equals 1 sc.
6. Work 5 blocks with red house and chimney, royal blue roof, windows, door and border. Work 4 blocks with med. blue house and chimney, red roof, windows,

door and border. Sections above and below house are all off-white.

Blocks (make 9):
Section 1:
Row 1: With off-white, ch 51, sc in 2nd ch from hook and in each ch across, turn. (50)
Rows 2-52: Ch 1, sc in next 8 sc, turn. (8)
At end of row 52, fasten off.

Section 2:
Following graph, start section 2 as indicated. Work windows and door with contrasting colors as indicated in Notes as work progresses in section 2.

Sections 3-8:
Following graph, start each section as indicated. Using colors indicated in Note 6, complete all blocks.

Assembly:
Sew blocks together alternating colors in

Continued on next page

Country Cottages

Continued from page 41

3 rows of 3 blocks each.

Border:

Following basic idea of sections 5-8, with med. blue and size H hook, work border around entire outer edge of afghan (see photo). Work section 5 on side of afghan (side of houses as on graph). Work section 6 across top of afghan. Work section 7 across side of afghan, and section 8 across bottom.❄

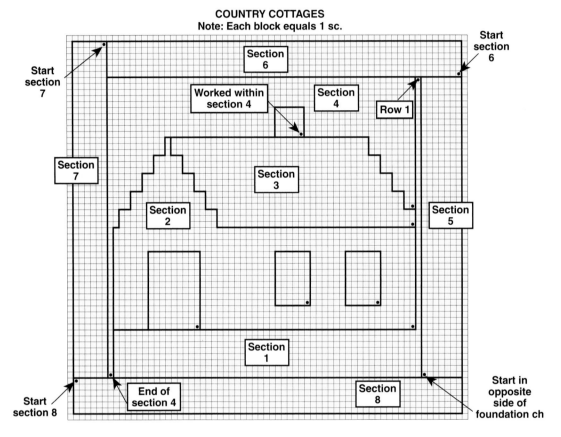

COUNTRY COTTAGES
Note: Each block equals 1 sc.

Chevron Shells

Continued from page 37

Across side 1: * Ch 3, sk over edge of dc or ch-3, sc in side edge of sc on end of next row, repeat from * across, ending with ch 3, (sc, ch 2, sc) in end ch.

Across top end: Ch 2, sk 2 ch, sc in next ch, [ch 1, sk 2 ch, (sc, ch 2, sc) in next ch, ch 1, sk 2 ch, sc in next ch] 2 times, ch 1, sk 3 ch, sc in next ch, * [ch 1, sk 2 ch, (sc, ch 2, sc) in next ch, ch 1, sk 2 ch, sc in next ch] 2 times, ch 3, sk 3 ch (over dcs), (sc, ch 2, sc) in ch-4 sp, ch 3, sk 3 ch, sc in next ch, [ch 1, sk 2 ch, (sc, ch 2, sc) in next ch, ch 1, sk 2 ch, sc in next ch] 2 times, ch 1, sk 3 ch, sc in next ch, repeat from * across, ending with ch 2, sk 2 ch, (sc, ch 2, sc) in last ch.

Across side 2: Repeat side 1, ending with ch 3, (sc, ch 2, sc) in beginning dc, sl st to join in 1st sc, fasten off.

Fringe:

For each fringe, cut six 16" strands of blue; fold strands in half, draw fold through st at bottom of afghan, draw cut ends through fold, pull to secure. Attach fringe at each ch at point and between. Trim fringe evenly.❄

Harlequin Tassels

Continued from page 38

in next 7 sts, turn.
Row 37: With coral, repeat row 31. (22)
Rows 38-42: Repeat rows 36-37. At end of row 42, fasten off lt. coral.
Row 43: Repeat row 31.
Rows 44-47: Repeat row 32.
Rows 48-107: Repeat rows 18-47.
Rows 108-121: Repeat rows 18-31.
Rows 122-126: Repeat row 32.
Row 127: Ch 3, dec 1 dc over next 2 dc, dc in each st across to within last 2 dc, dec 1 dc over last 2 dc, turn. (20)
Rows 128-135: Repeat row 127. (4)
Row 136: (Dec 1 dc over next 2 dc) twice. (2)
Row 137: Dec 1 dc over 2 sts, fasten off.

Edging:
Join lt. coral in end ch of row 1, ch 1, 4 sc in same point, working up side edge, sc evenly spaced up edge to top point, 4 sc in top point, sc evenly spaced down opposite edge, join, fasten off.

Light Coral Panel (make 3):
Rows 1-17: With lt. coral, repeat rows 1-17 of coral panel.
Rows 18-19: Ch 3, dc in each dc across, turn.
Rows 20-26: Reversing yarn colors, repeat rows 36-37 of coral panel.
Row 27: With lt. coral, repeat row 31 of coral panel.
Rows 28-31: With lt. coral, ch 3, dc in each dc across, turn.
Rows 32-91: Reversing yarn colors, repeat rows 18-47 of coral panel.
Rows 92-117: Reversing yarn colors, repeat rows 18-43 of coral panel.
Rows 118-126: With lt. coral, ch 3, dc in each st across, turn.
Rows 127-137: With lt. coral, repeat rows 127-137 of coral panel.

Edging:
With coral, repeat edging of coral panel.

Assembly:
Holding right sides together and alternating panels, working in back lps only, join

lt. coral in sc opposite row 12 of panel, ch 1, sc evenly spaced along edge, ending in sc opposite row 127 of panel; fasten off.
Join remaining panels in same manner, beginning and ending with coral panel.

Tassels:
For each tassel, cut sixteen 14" strands. Cut a strand of yarn and tie tightly at center of strands. Fold strands at center; cut a 12" strand and wrap several times around strands 1" down from top; weave in end to secure.
Matching tassel colors to panels, attach tassel to each point.❈

Purrfectly Pretty
Instructions on page 35

COLOR KEY	
☐	MC
◼	CC

PURRFECTLY PRETTY

Row 41

Row 1

These stunning snowflake blocks are crocheted together as you work, creating a fabulous afghan that will make your home sparkle with holiday cheer.

Christmas Snowflakes

By
ROSALIE DEVRIES

Skill Level
Challenging

Size
42" x 59"; block = 8" x 8"

Materials
4-ply worsted-weight yarn: 15 oz. bright red,
8 oz. bright green, 5 oz. white
Hook size F/5 (4.00mm)

Gauge
4 sc = 1"

Instructions

Motif (make 35):
Rnd 1: With green, ch 5, join with sl st to form ring, (ch 5, dc in 4th ch from hook) 3 times, sc in ch between 1st and 2nd repeat, ch 4, dc in 4th ch from hook, sc in ring, * ch 4, dc in 4th ch from hook, repeat from (to) 2 times, sc in ch between 1st and 2nd ch-lp, ch 4, dc in 4th ch from hook, sc in ring, repeat from * 4 times, join with sl st in 1st ch of beginning ch-5, fasten off. (6 arms)

Rnd 2: Join white in 1st ch-lp of rnd 1, ch 5, * dc in 4th ch from hook, sc in next ch-lp, (ch 4, dc in 4th ch from hook) 2 times, sc in next ch-1 sp at end of arm, repeat from (to) 2 times, sc in next ch-lp, ch 4, dc in 4th ch from hook, sc in next 2 ch-lps, ch 4, repeat from * around, join with sl st in 1st ch of beginning ch-5, fasten off.

Rnd 3: Join red in 2nd ch-lp of rnd 2, ch 7, dc in 4th ch from hook, * sc in next ch-lp, ch 4, dc in 4th ch from hook, sc in next ch-lp, ch 4, dc in 4th ch from hook, dc in next ch-lp, ch 4, dc in 4th ch from hook, sk next 2 ch-lps, dc in next ch-lp, ch 4, dc in 4th ch from hook, repeat from * around, join with sl st in 3rd ch of beginning ch-7.

Rnd 4: Sl st to 1st lp, ch 2, 3 hdc in lp, ch 1, 4 sc in next lp, * ch 1, 4 hdc in next lp, ch 1, 4 dc in next lp, ch 1, 7 tr in next lp (corner), ch 1, 4 dc in next lp, ch 1, 4 hdc in next lp, ch 1, 4 sc in next lp, rep from * around, join with sl st in top of ch-2, fasten off.

Rnd 5 (first motif only): [Join green in 3rd tr of corner 7-tr group, ch 10, * sk next tr, sc in next tr, (ch 5, sc in next ch-1 sp) 6 times, ch 5, sc in 3rd tr of next corner group], ch 9, repeat from * around, join with sl st in 1st ch of ch-10, fasten off.

Rnd 5 (joining rnd for remaining motifs): Repeat from [to] of rnd 5 for first motif, ch 4, sc in 5th ch of corner ch-9 of first motif, ch 4, sk next tr of 2nd motif, sc in next tr, * ch 2, sc in 3rd ch of ch-5 of 1st motif, ch 2, sc in ch-1 sp of

Continued on page 49

Inspired by the classic Amish quilt pattern, "Sunshine and Shadow," this vivid afghan brings the brilliant shades of summer into any room of your home.

Summer Picnic

By
KATHERINE ENG

Skill Level
Average

Size
46" square

Materials
4-ply worsted-weight yarn: 17½ oz. dark blue, 10½ oz. forest green, 7 oz. each bright blue and country red, 3½ oz. each bright green, lavender, dark turquoise and turquoise
Hook size F/5 (4.00mm)

Gauge
1 small square = 1¼" across

Instructions

Rnd 1: With country red, ch 5, join with sl st to form ring, ch 4, retaining last lp of each tr on hook, 2 tr in ring, yo, draw through all 3 lps on hook, ch 3, (retaining last lp of each tr on hook, 3 tr in ring, yo, draw through all 4 lps on hook, ch 3) 7 times, join with sl st in top of ch-4. (8 petals)

Rnd 2: Ch 1, sc in center tr of 1st petal, 2 sc in ch-3 sp, * (sc, ch 2, sc) in top of next tr cluster for corner, 2 sc in next ch-3 sp, repeat from * 3 times, (sc, ch 2, sc) in top of next tr cluster for corner, 2 sc in next ch-3 sp, join with sl st in 1st sc. (28 sc)

Rnd 3: Ch 1, sc in each sc around with (sc, ch 3, sc) in each corner sp, join with sl st in 1st sc, fasten off. (36 sc)

Note: *From this point, the word "RND" refers to an indicated color. Work around the outer perimeter of the afghan, creating rectangles and squares, ending after the completion of Rnd 16.*

RND 1: (See center block diagram.) Join brt. blue with sl st in any corner sp.

Row 1 (right side): Ch 6, sc in 2nd ch from hook, (ch 1, sk 1 ch, sc in next ch) 2 times, sl st in same corner ch-3 sp, sl st up to 1st sc, turn.

Row 2: Ch 1, sc in 1st sc, (ch 1, sk ch-1 sp, sc in next sc) 2 times, turn.

Row 3: Ch 1, sc in 1st sc, (ch 1, sk ch-1 sp, sc in next sc) 2 times, sl st to next sc on center square, sl st up to next sc, turn. Repeat rows 2-3 until 11 rows are completed, ending with sl st in corner ch-3 sp on center square.

Repeat Rnd 1, rows 1-11, for remaining 3 sides. Fasten off.

RND 2: Join brt. green with sl st in right-hand end sc at top of any 11th row of blue rectangle.

Row 1 (right side): Ch 1, sc in sc, (ch 1, sk ch-1 sp, sc in next sc) 2 times, sl st to 1st foundation ch of blue rectangle on left, sl st in next ch-1 sp, turn.

Continued on next page

Summer Picnic

Continued from page 47

Row 2: Ch 1, sc in sc, (ch 1, sk ch-1 sp, sc in next sc) 2 times, turn.

Rep pattern stitch until 5 rows are completed to form a square. Repeat rows 1-11 of Rnd 1, joining each row with sl st to corresponding side rows of 1st rectangle. Continue rnd in same manner until 4 rectangles and 4 squares are complete. Fasten off.

Note: *For Rnds 3-16, the number in parentheses indicates the number of squares between each rectangle. Always add 1 square each rnd between rectangles.*

RND 3: With country red, work as for Rnd 2, adding 1 square between rectangles. (2)

RNDS 4-16: Work each row as for Rnd 3, using the following colors for the following rows:

RND 4: Dk. turquoise (3).
RND 5: Turquoise (4).
RND 6: Lavender (5).
RND 7: Brt. blue (6).
RND 8: Forest green (7).
RND 9: Dk. blue (8).
RND 10: Country red (9).
RND 11: Brt. blue (10).
RND 12: Brt. green (11).
RND 13: Country red (12).
RND 14: Dk. turquoise (13).
RND 15: Turquoise (14).
RND 16: Lavender (15).

SUMMER PICNIC

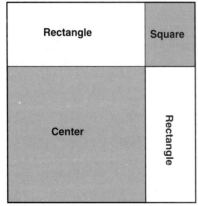

Center Block Diagram

Fill-Ins and Triangular Corners:

Note: Fill-ins are worked across sides of afghan and triangular corners are worked at corners.

Fill-Ins:

Row 1 (right side): Join brt. blue in end sc of any corner rectangle, ch 1, 5 sc down left-hand side of corner rectangle, sl st to next square as on previous pattern, sl st up 1 row, turn.

Row 2: Ch 1, sc in next 3 sc, dec 1 sc over next 2 sc, turn.

Row 3: Ch 1, dec 1 sc over next 2 sts, sc in next 2 sc, sl st as before, turn.

Row 4: Ch 1, sc in next sc, dec 1 sc over next 2 sc, turn.

Row 5: Ch 1, dec 1 sc over next 2 sc, sl st in top of next square. Repeat pattern to next corner of afghan. After last row of last square, sl st in end ch of next corner rectangle. Do not fasten off.

Corner Triangle:

Row 1 (right side): Ch 1, sc in end ch and sides of sts across rectangle, turn. (12 sc)

Rows 2-5: Ch 1, dec 1 sc over next 2 sc, sc in each sc across to within last 2 sc, dec 1 sc over next 2 sc, turn. (4)

Row 6: Ch 1, (dec 1 sc over next 2 sc) 2 times, turn. (2)

Row 7: Ch 1, dec 1 sc over next 2 sc, fasten off. (1)

Join brt. blue in end sc of next rectangle, repeat fill-ins and corner triangles around remaining outer edge of afghan.

At end of last corner, ch 1, * 9 sc down left-hand side of corner triangle, 7 sc across each fill-in, 9 sc across side of next corner triangle, 3 sc in corner sc, repeat from * around, join, fasten off.

Border #1:

Rnd 1: Join forest green in any sc on edge, ch 1, sc in each sc around with 3 sc in each center corner st, join with sl st in 1st sc.

Rnd 2: Ch 2, hdc in each sc around with 3 hdc in each center corner st, join with sl st in top of ch-2, turn.

Rnd 3: Ch 1, sc in same hdc as ch-1, sc

in each hdc around with 3 sc in each center corner st, join with sl st in 1st sc, turn.
Rnds 4-7: Repeat rnds 2-3.
Rnd 8: Repeat rnd 2, fasten off.

Border #2:
Rnd 1 (right side): Counting corner st as 1 st, join dk. blue in 5th st to the left of any corner st, ch 1, sc in each st around with 3 sc in each center corner st, join with sl st in 1st sc.
Rnd 2: Ch 3, 4 dc in same st, (sk 2 sc, sc in next sc, sk 2 sc, 5 dc in next sc) around with (sk 1 sc, 5 dc in center corner st, sk 1 sc, sc in next sc, sk 2 sc, 5 dc in next sc) in corners, adjusting number of stitches skipped at corners if necessary to make work come out even at corners; end with sc, join with sl st to top of ch-3, turn.
Rnd 3: Ch 3, 4 dc in same st, (sc in 2nd dc of 5-dc group, 5 dc in center dc, sc in next dc) for corner, (5 dc in next sc, sc in center dc of 5-dc group) around, join with sl st in top of ch-3, turn.
Note: Rnds 4-9 of border #2 are repeats of rnd 3 with changes for corners only.

Rnd 4: Sl st to next sc, ch 3, (sc, ch 3, sc) in center dc of 5 dc at corner.
Rnd 5: Work 7 dc in corner ch-3 sp.
Rnd 6: Sc in 2nd dc of 7-dc group, 5 dc in center dc, sc in 6th dc of same 7-dc group.
Rnd 7: Repeat corners as for rnd 4.
Rnd 8: Repeat corners as for rnd 5.
Rnd 9: Repeat corners as for rnd 6.
At end of rnd 9, turn.
Rnd 10 (right side): Ch 2, (dc in next sc, hdc in next dc, sc in next 3 dc, hdc in next dc) around, with (dc in 1st and 2nd dc, 5 dc in center dc, dc in 4th and 5th dc) for corner, end with join with sl st in top of ch-2.
Rnd 11: Ch 1, sc in each st around with 3 sc in each center corner st, join with sl st in 1st sc, fasten off.

Border #3:
Rnd 1 (right side): With country red, repeat rnd 1 of border #1, turn.
Rnds 2-3: Ch 1, sc in each sc around with 3 sc in each center corner st, join with sl st in 1st sc, turn.
At end of rnd 3, fasten off.❄

Christmas Snowflakes

Continued from page 44

2nd motif, repeat from * 6 times, ch 2, sc in 3rd ch of ch-5 of 1st motif, ch 2, sc in 3rd tr of corner group of 2nd motif, ch 4, sc in 5th ch of ch-9 of 1st motif, ch 4, sk next tr of 2nd motif, sc in next tr, (to join 2 sides, repeat from first * once), complete as rnd 5 of 1st motif, fasten off.
Join motifs to form afghan 5 x 7 motifs.

Border:
Rnd 1: Join green in corner lp, ch 1, * 7 sc in corner lp, 4 sc in each lp to next corner, repeat from * around, join with sl st in 1st sc, fasten off.

Rnd 2: Join white in any sc in rnd 1, ch 1, sc in same sc, * sc in each sc to 4th sc of 7-sc corner group, 3 sc in 4th sc, repeat from * around, join with sl st in 1st sc, fasten off.
Rnd 3: Join red in any sc on rnd 2, ch 1, sc in same sc, * sc in each sc to center sc in corner, 3 sc in corner, repeat from * around, join with sl st in 1st sc, fasten off.
Rnd 4: Join green in any sc on rnd 3, * ch 1, sk next sc, sl st in next sc, ch 1, sk next sc, insert hook from back to front in next sc, sl st, repeat from * around, join with sl st in 1st ch-1, fasten off.❄

The Blessed Event

Soft and pretty baby afghans are perennial favorites among crocheters. Fun to make in pastels or bright shades, they're as practical as they are beautiful, and afghans are always much appreciated at baby showers. Welcome the new baby into your circle of friends and family with a lovingly handmade gift that's sure to be a warm and cozy comfort at home or on the go.

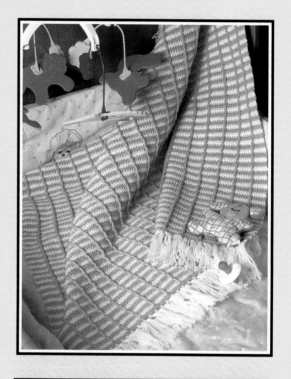

Cloud-soft stripes are highlighted with raised bars for textural interest in this sweetheart of a baby afghan. Create it in your favorite baby pastel and white for a beautiful gift.

Baby Blue Stripes

By
ALINE SUPLINSKAS

Skill Level
Easy

Size
38" x 35"

Materials
Pompadour yarn: 8 oz. each white and light blue
Hook size F/5 (4.00mm)

Gauge
5 sc = 1"; 5 sc rows = 1"

Instructions

Row 1: With white, ch 169, sc in 2nd ch from hook and in each ch across, turn. (168)

Row 2: Ch 1, sc in each sc across to within last sc, draw up a lp in last sc, drop white, pull lt. blue through last 2 lps on hook, turn.

Row 3: Ch 1, sc in next 6 sts, (yo, insert hook from right to left behind next ch of foundation ch, draw up a lp, complete as for dc, sk 1 st, sc in next 6 sts) across, turn.

Row 4: Repeat row 2, change to white in last st.

Rows 5-6: Ch 1, sc in each sc across, turn.

Row 7: Ch 1, sc in next 6 sts, (yo twice, insert hook from front to back to front around post of post st, draw up lp, work off st as a tr, sk 1 st, sc in next 6 sts) across, turn.

Row 8: Repeat row 4.

Rows 9-10: Repeat rows 5-6.

Row 11: Ch 1, sc in next 6 sts, (tr around post of fptr, sk 1 st, sc in next 6 sts) across, turn.

Row 12: Repeat row 4.

Repeat rows 9-12 until afghan measures 31" in length, ending with row 12.

Trim:

Row 1: Join white in upper right corner, ch 1, sc in same st, (ch 2, sk 2 sts, sc in next st) across, fasten off. Join white in opposite side of foundation ch, ch 1, sc in same ch, (ch 2, sk 2 sts, sc in next ch) across, fasten off.

Fringe:

For each fringe, cut four 8" strands white, fold in half, insert hook in 1st ch-2 sp, pull fold through st, pull cut ends through lp; tighten. Fringe in each ch-2 sp on each end of afghan.❀

Precious puff-stitch rocking horses and hearts adorn each panel on this warm and comfy baby blanket. Choose your favorite accent colors for a special gift.

Rocking Horses

By
BOBBI HAYWARD

Skill Level
Average

Size
36" x 50" plus fringe

Materials
4-ply worsted-weight yarn: 24½ oz. white,
7 oz. each baby pink, baby blue and yellow
Afghan hook size K (14"), hook size K/10½ (6.50mm)

Gauge
14 sts and 11 rows = 4" in afghan st

Instructions

Notes:
1. BAS (Basic Afghan Stitch): Each row is worked in two parts, pulling up lps and working them off the hook.
Row 1: Using afghan hook, ch desired length. Keeping all lps on hook, pull up a lp in 2nd ch from hook and in each ch across; yo and draw through 1 lp, (yo and draw through 2 lps) until only 1 lp remains on hook. Last lp on hook is 1st lp of next row. Do not turn work.
Row 2: Keeping all lps on hook, draw up a lp in 2nd vertical bar and in each verti-cal bar across, yo and draw through 1 lp, (yo and draw through 2 lps) until 1 lp remains.
Repeat row 2 for BAS.
2. PS (Puff Stitch): Yo, draw up a lp under next bar in 2nd row below working row, yo and draw through 2 lps on hook, (yo, draw up a lp under same bar below, yo and draw through 2 lps on hook) 2 times, yo and draw through 3 lps on hook.

Center Panel:
Rows 1-4: With afghan hook and white, ch 26, work even according to BAS instructions above.
Row 5: Draw up a lp under each of next 6 bars, * PS, draw up a lp under next bar, repeat from * 4 times, work PS, draw up a lp under each of remaining 8 bars of working row (26 lps on hook and 6 PS in row below), complete row.
Row 6: Draw up a lp under each of next 5 bars (6 lps on hook), PS, draw up a lp under each of next 11 bars, PS, draw up a lp under each of remaining 7 bars (26 lps on hook), complete row.
Rows 7-35: Working from Chart A, begin with row 7 of chart and work through row 35.
Rows 36-134: Repeat rows 3-35 of chart 3 times (4 rocking horse/heart repeats in all). At end of last row, fasten off.

Right Edging:
Row 1: With right side up and foundation-
Continued on page 56

Rocking Horses

Continued from page 54

ch edge to the right, with crochet hook, join pink in ch at upper right corner, ch 1, sc in same st, sc around 2 horizontal strands (which are now vertical) of 1st st from edge in next row, * dc around 2 horizontal strands of 2nd st from edge in each of next 2 rows, sc around 2 horizontal strands of first st in each of next 3 rows, repeat from * across, ending with dc around 2 horizontal strands of the 2nd st from edge in each of next 2 rows, sc around 2 horizontal strands of 1st st from edge in last row, sc in sp between last row of sts and fastened-off edge, turn. (136)

Row 2: Ch 1, sc in each st across, turn.

Row 3: Ch 1, sc in each of 1st 5 sc, PS around post of next sc in 2nd row below (2nd sc of 3-sc group) and complete PS by working yo, draw through all 4 lps on hook (instead of 3 lps), * sc in each of next 4 sc, PS around post of next sc in 2nd row below, repeat from * to within last 5 sc, sc in last 5 sc, turn. (26 PS)

Row 4: Repeat row 2; fasten off pink, turn.

Row 5: Join blue with sl st in 1st sc, ch 1, sc in same st, sc in next sc, * dc around posts of next 2 sc in 2nd row below, sc in each of next 3 sc, repeat from * across; end with dc around post of next 2 sc in 2nd row below, sc in each of last 2 sc, turn.

Rows 6-8: Repeat rows 2-4. At end of row 8, fasten off.

Row 9: With yellow, repeat row 5.

Row 10: Repeat row 2.

Row 11: Repeat row 3, fasten off.

Left Edging:
Holding same panel right side up with fastened-off edge to the right and side edge across top, with crochet hook, join pink with sl st in fastened-off st at upper right corner, ch 1, work 11 rows of edging as for right edging.

Left and Right Panels:
Work as for center panel; complete edg-ings as indicated below.

Left Panel, Right Edging:
Holding panel right side up with foundation-ch edge to the right and side edge across top, with crochet hook, join pink with sl st in ch at upper right corner, ch 1. Repeat rows 1-11 of center panel right edging. Fasten off.

Left Panel, Left Edging:
Holding panel right side up with fastened-off edge to the right and side edge across top, with crochet hook, attach yellow with sl st in fastened-off st at upper right corner, ch 1. Repeat rows 1-4 of of center panel right edging. Fasten off.

Right Panel, Right Edging:
Holding panel right side up with foundation-ch edge to the right and side edge across top, with crochet hook, join yellow with sl st in ch at upper right corner, ch 1. Repeat rows 1-4 of of center panel right edging. Fasten off.

Right Panel, Left Edging:
Holding panel right side up with fastened-off edge to the right and side edge across top, with crochet hook, attach pink with sl st in fastened-off st at upper right corner, ch 1. Repeat rows 1-11 of center panel right edging. Fasten off.

Assembly:
Place two panels side by side with right side up and fastened-off edges at top. Hold yellow at back of work and work sl sts on right side, alternating edge to edge as follows:

With crochet hook, join yellow with sl st in st at bottom edge of right panel. Insert hook from right side of panel into 1st st at bottom edge of left panel, hook yarn from beneath, draw through work and through lp on hook (sl st made).

Work another sl st in same st as before on right panel, then sl st in next st on left panel.

Continue working in this manner — alter-

nating sl sts from panel to panel and being careful to keep puff sts properly aligned — until panels are joined. Fasten off.
Join remaining panel in same manner.

Fringe (optional):
For each fringe, cut eight 11" strands of yarn; fold strands in half, draw fold through st at bottom of afghan, draw cut ends through fold, pull to secure. Attach 1 fringe into center of each pink and blue stripe. Attach 1 fringe at each side into center of yellow edge. Attach 2 fringes evenly spaced in each yellow double stripe between panels. Attach 5 fringes evenly spaced in each white panel.
If no fringe is added, work a row of sc across each end of afghan.❈

STITCH KEY

■ Puff stitch (ps)

ROCKING HORSES

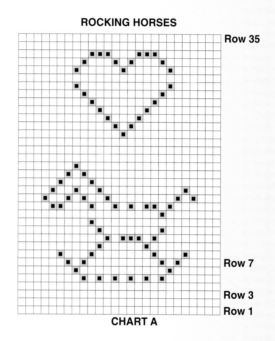

Row 35

Row 7

Row 3
Row 1

CHART A

Dimensional flowers grace the corners of this shell-stitch baby afghan in bright baby colors. It's fast and easy to make in worsted-weight yarn.

Baby's Posies

By
GLENDA WINKLEMAN

Skill Level
Easy

Size
31" x 46"

Materials
4-ply worsted-weight yarn: 18 oz. pink,
3 oz. each baby yellow, baby blue and baby green
Hook size I/9 (6.00mm)

Gauge
1 shell st = 1"; 3 rows = 2"

Instructions

Note: Shell: (2 dc, ch 2, 2 dc) in same place.

Center:
Row 1: With pink, ch 45, shell in 3rd ch from hook, * sk 2 ch, shell in next ch, repeat from * across, turn. (15 shells)
Rows 2-58: Sl st into ch-2 sp of 1st shell, ch 3, (dc, ch 2, 2 dc) in same sp, shell in ch-2 sp of each shell across, fasten off pink at end of row 58.

Border:
Rnd 59: Join yellow in top right corner, ch 3, (dc, ch 2, 2 dc) in same st (beginning shell made), * shell in ch-2 sp of each shell across, (2 dc, ch 2, 2 dc, ch 2, 2 dc) in corner shell; working down side, shell in ch-2 sp of last shell in every other row, (2 dc, ch 2, 2 dc, ch 2, 2 dc) in corner, repeat from * around, join with sl st in top of ch-3, fasten off.
Rnd 60: Join blue in ch-2 sp of any shell, beginning shell in same sp, shell in ch-2 sp of each shell around, do not work corners as in rnd 59, join with sl st in top of ch-3, fasten off.

Rnd 61: Join green in ch-2 sp of any shell, beginning shell in same sp, * shell in ch-2 sp of each shell around with 1 shell between shells at each corner (corner st made), repeat from * around, join with sl st in top of ch-3, fasten off.
Rnd 62: With pink, repeat rnd 60. Continue in rows.
Rows 63-66: With pink, start in right bottom corner in ch-2 sp of corner st, shell in each shell across to top right corner st, shell in corner st, turn. Work back and forth for a total of 5 rows pink counting row 62, fasten off.
Rows 67-70: Repeat rows 63-66 on opposite side; fasten off.
Rnd 71: Start in right bottom corner with yellow, * shell in ch-2 sp of each shell across, with (2 dc, ch 2, 2 dc, ch 2, 2 dc) in corner st, shell in every other end shell ch-2 sp across 4 odd rows, shell in every shell across row, repeat shell in every other end shell ch-2 sp across 4 odd rows, repeat

Continued on page 65

This cuddly crib blanket is so much fun to make, you'll want to make several for shower gifts. Variegated baby yarn is softened with pale yellow, white and blue.

Baby Shells

By
KATHERINE ENG

Skill Level
Easy

Size
35" x 43"

Materials
Baby yarn: 10½ oz. baby tweed or variegated,
3½ oz. each yellow and blue, 7 oz. white
Hook size F/5 (4.00mm)

Gauge
4 sc = 1"; 2 sc rows = ½"; 3 shell rows = 1½"

Instructions

Notes:
1. Work with 2 strands held together throughout: 1 strand tweed or variegated and 1 strand color indicated.
2. Rows 4 and 5 establish pattern used throughout center and on parts of border.
3. To add new color, fasten off 1st color and attach new color before drawing through last lp of last st at end of row.
4. Do not fasten off tweed except as specified on border.

Row 1 (right side): With blue and tweed, ch 116, sc in 2nd ch from hook and in each ch across, turn. (115)
Row 2: Ch 1, sc in each sc across, turn.
Row 3: Ch 1, sc in 1st sc, [sk 2 sc, (2 dc, ch 2, 2 dc) in next sc (shell made), sk 2 sc, sc in next sc] across, ending with sk 2 sc, sc in last sc, turn.
Row 4: Ch 3, dc in same sc, (sc in ch-2 sp of next shell, shell in next sc) across, ending with 2 dc in last sc, turn.
Row 5: Ch 1, sc in 1st dc, (shell in next sc,

sc in ch-2 sp of next shell) across, ending with sc in top of ch-3, turn.
Rows 6-89: Working 3 rows white, 3 rows yellow, 3 rows white and 3 rows blue, repeat rows 4-5 until 29 patterns of shell stripes are complete (87 rows of shells plus 2 beginning sc rows = 89 rows). Do not fasten off, turn.
Row 90 (wrong side): Continuing with blue and tweed, ch 3, (hdc in next dc, sc in next dc, sc in next ch-2 sp, sc in next dc, hdc in next dc, dc in next sc) across, turn.
Row 91: Ch 1, sc in each st across, fasten off.

Border:
With right side up, join white and tweed in side of top of dc to the left of corner ch on long edge, 5 sts from corner. (Each dc counts as 2 sts; each sc as 1 st.)
Rnd 1: Working down long side, ch 1, * sc in top of dc, sc over side edge of sc, sc over base of next dc, repeat from * to cor-

Continued on page 65

Delicate rings of baby pink and pale blue shells bring out the unusual shape of this lacy blanket. Beautiful in either carriage or crib, this afghan will be Baby's favorite.

Shells in the Round

By
DELLA BRENNEISE

Skill Level
Average

Size
34" in diameter

Materials
3-ply sport-weight yarn: 7 oz. white,
2 oz. baby blue, 1 oz. baby pink
Hook size H/8 (5.00mm)

Gauge
6 rnds of shells = 3"

Instructions

Rnd 1: With white, ch 6, join with sl st to form ring, ch 1, 16 sc in ring, join with sl st in 1st sc. (16)

Rnd 2: [Ch 4, sk next sc, sc in next sc] 7 times, ch 2, dc in beginning of rnd.

Rnd 3: [Ch 4, sc in next ch-lp] 7 times, ch 2, dc in top of dc.

Rnd 4: [Ch 5, sc in next ch-lp] 7 times, ch 5, sl st in top of dc.

Rnd 5: Sl st into ch-5 sp, ch 3 (first dc), 5 dc in same ch-sp, [6 dc in next ch-sp] around, join with sl st in top of ch-3.

Rnd 6: Ch 1, sc in same st, [ch 3, sk 1 dc, sc in next dc] around, ending with ch 1, hdc in 1st sc. (24 lps)

Rnd 7: [Ch 3, sc in next ch-lp] around, ending with ch 1, hdc in top of hdc.

Rnd 8: [Ch 4, sc in next ch-lp] around, ending with ch 4, sl st in top of hdc.

Rnd 9: Sl st into next ch-sp, ch 3 (first dc), [dc, ch 2, 2 dc] in same sp (beginning shell made), * ch 2, sc in next ch sp, ch 2, [2 dc, ch 2, 2 dc] in next ch sp (shell made), repeat from * around, ending with sl st in top of ch-3.

Rnd 10: Sl st into ch-2 sp, beginning shell in same sp, [ch 1, sc in ch-2 sp, ch 2, sc in next ch-2 sp, ch 1, shell in next shell] around, ending with ch 1, sc in ch-2 sp, ch 2, sc in next ch-2 sp, ch 1, join with sl st in top of ch-3, fasten off.

Rnd 11: Join pink with sl st in ch-2 sp of any shell, beginning shell in same sp, [shell in next ch-2 sp, shell in next shell] around, ending with shell in next ch-2 sp, join, fasten off.

Rnd 12: Join white between any 2 shells, beginning shell in same sp, * sc in ch-2 sp of shell, shell between next 2 shells, repeat from * around, ending with sc in top of shell, join.

Rnd 13: Sl st into ch-2 sp of shell, beginning shell in same sp, sc in each sc and shell in each shell around, ending with sc in last sc, join.

Rnd 14: Repeat rnd 13, fasten off.

Rnd 15: Join blue in any sc, ch 5, 5 dc in same st, * sc in ch-2 sp of next shell, 6 dc in next sc (scallop made), repeat from * around, ending with sc in ch-2 sp, join, fasten off.

Continued on next page

Shells in the Round

Continued from page 63

Rnd 16: Join white in any sc between scallops, beginning shell in same st, * sc in 3rd dc, ch 1, sc in 4th dc, shell in next sc, repeat from * around, ending with sc in 3rd dc, ch 1, sc in 4th dc, join.

Rnd 17: Sl st into ch-2 sp, beginning shell in same sp, * shell in next ch-1 sp, shell in next shell, repeat from * around, ending with shell in ch-1 sp, join.

Rnd 18: Sl st into ch-2 sp of shell, sc in same sp, * ch 1, shell in next shell, ch 1, sc in ch-2 sp of next shell, repeat from * around, join.

Rnd 19: Sc in ch-1 sp, * ch 2, shell in next shell, [ch 2, sc in ch-1 sp] 2 times, repeat from * around, ending with shell in next shell, ch 2, sc in ch-1 sp, ch 2, join, fasten off.

Rnd 20: Join pink in ch-2 sp of any shell, beginning shell in same sp, * sk ch-2 sp, shell in next ch-2 sp, ch 2, shell in next shell, repeat from * around, ending with shell in next ch-2 sp, join, fasten off.

Rnd 21: Join white between any 2 shells, beginning shell in same sp, * sc in ch-2 sp of shell, shell in sp between shells, repeat from * around, ending with sc in ch-2 sp of shell, join.

Rnds 22-26: Repeat rnd 21. At end of rnd 26, fasten off.

Rnd 27: Join blue in any sc, ch 3, 5 dc in same sp, * sc in ch-2 sp of next shell, 6 dc in next sc, repeat from * around, ending with sc in sc, join, fasten off.

Rnd 28: Join white in any sc, beginning shell in same st, * sc in 3rd dc, ch 1, sc in next dc, shell in sc between scallops, repeat from * around, ending with sc in 3rd dc, ch 1, sc in next dc, join.

Rnd 29: Sl st into ch-2 sp, beginning shell in same sp, * shell in ch-1 sp, shell in next shell, repeat from * around, ending with final shell, join.

Rnd 30: Sl st into ch-2 sp, beginning shell in same sp, * sc in ch-2 sp of next shell, shell in next shell, repeat from * around, ending with shell in ch-2 sp, join.

Rnd 31: Sl st into ch-2 sp, beginning shell in same sp, * ch 1, sc in next sc, ch 1, shell in next shell, repeat from * around, ending with ch 1, sc in next sc, ch 1, join.

Rnd 32: Repeat rnd 31.

Rnd 33: Sl st into ch-2 sp, beginning shell in same sp, * sc in ch-1 sp, ch 2, sc in ch-1 sp, shell in next shell, repeat from * around, ending with sc in ch-1 sp, ch 2, sc in ch-1 sp, join, fasten off.

Rnd 34: Join pink in ch-2 sp of any shell, beginning shell in same sp, * shell in next ch-2 sp, shell in next shell, repeat from * around, ending with shell in ch-2 sp, join, fasten off.

Rnd 35: Join white between any 2 shells, ch 3, 2 dc in same sp, * sc in ch-2 sp of next shell, 3 dc between next 2 shells, repeat from * around, ending with sc in ch-2 sp of shell, join.

Rnd 36: Sl st in next dc, ch 3, 2 dc in same st, * sc in next sc, sk next dc, 3 dc in next dc, repeat from * around, join.

Rnd 37: Sl st in next dc, ch 3, 3 dc in same st, * sc in next sc, sk next dc, 4 dc in next dc, repeat from * around, ending with sc in next sc, join.

Rnd 38: Sl st in next 2 dc, beginning shell in same dc, * sc in sc, sk dc, 2 dc in next dc, ch 2, 2 dc in next dc, repeat from * around, join, fasten off.

Fringe:
For each fringe, cut four 8" strands of yarn; fold strands in half, draw fold through st at bottom of afghan, draw cut ends through fold, pull to secure. Attach fringe in each ch-2 sp around on rnd 38. Trim ends evenly.❁

Baby's Posies

Continued from page 59

corner st, repeat from * around, join with sl st in top of ch-3, fasten off.

Rnd 72: With blue, repeat rnd 60.
Rnd 73: With green, repeat rnd 61.
Rnd 74: With pink, repeat rnd 60, fasten off.

Flower (make 2):
Rnd 1: With yellow, ch 5, join with sl st to form ring, 5 sc in ring, join with sl st in 1st sc.
Rnd 2: Ch 3, dc in same st, 2 dc in each st around, join with sl st in top of ch-3, fasten off.
Rnd 3: Join blue in any dc, ch 4, 4 tr in same st, 5 tr in each st around, join with sl st in top of ch-4, fasten off.

Flower Center (make 2):
Rnd 1: With pink, ch 5, join with sl st to form ring, 6 sc in ring, join with sl st in 1st sc, fasten off.

Leaves:
Rnd 1: Join green to bottom back of any tr on flower, ch 12, sc in 2nd ch from hook, dc in each of next 5 ch, tr in each of next 4 ch, sc in last ch, turn, working up other side of foundation ch, sc in last ch again, tr in each of next 4 ch, dc in each of next 5 ch, sc in last ch, fasten off. Turn flower and work another leaf in position shown in photo.

Assembly:
Attach flower center to center of each flower. Attach flowers to left top corner and right bottom corner of center section as shown in photo.❀

Baby Shells

Continued from page 60

ner, (sc, ch 2, sc) in corner st, sc in each st across to next corner, (sc, ch 2, sc) in corner, repeat from * on long side, (sc, ch 2, sc) in corner, sc in each st across, join with sl st in 1st sc, turn.
Rnd 2: Ch 1, sc in next sc and in each sc around, with (sc, ch 2, sc) in each corner ch-2 sp, join, turn.
Rnds 3-4: Repeat rnd 2.
Note: At bottom and top only of rnd 5, sk 3 sc after shell twice to make pattern come out evenly at corners.
Rnd 5: Ch 1, sc in next sc, (sk 2 sc, shell in next sc, sk 2 sc, sc in next sc) around, with (sk 1 sc, shell in corner ch-2 sp, sk 2 sc, sc in next sc) in corners, join with sl st in 1st sc, turn. (19 shells across top and bottom between corner shells and 23 shells across sides between corner shells)
Rnds 6-7: Sl st into ch-2 sp of shell, ch 1, (sc in ch-2 sp, shell in next sc) around, with (sc in 2nd dc of corner shell, shell in ch-2 sp, sc in next dc) in corners, at end of rnd, join with sl st in 1st sc, turn. At end of rnd 7, fasten off.
Rnd 8: Join yellow and tweed in any ch-2 sp on edge, ch 3 (counts as 1st dc of shell), (shell in ch-2 sp, dc in next sc) around, with (3 dc, ch 2, 3 dc) in each corner, join with sl st in top of ch-3, turn.
Rnd 9: Sl st in dc, ch 3, (shell in dc, sc in ch-2 sp of shell) around, with (sc in 2nd dc of shell, shell in corner ch-2 sp, sk 1 dc, sc in next dc) in corners, join with sl st in top of ch-3, turn.
Rnd 10: Sl st in sc, ch 3, (shell in sc, sc in ch-2 sp of shell) around, working corners as for rnd 6, join with sl st in top of ch-3, fasten off, turn.
Rnd 11: With white and tweed, repeat rnd 8.
Rnd 12: Ch 1, sc in next st and in each st around, with (sc, ch 2, sc) in each ch-2 sp, joining blue, join with sl st in 1st sc, fasten off white, do not turn.
Rnd 13: * Ch 3, (sl st, ch 3, sl st) in ch-2 sp of shell, ch 3, sl st in center sc between shells, repeat from * around, with [ch 2, sk 1 sc, (sl st, ch 3, sl st) in next sc, ch 3, (sl st, ch 3, sl st, ch 5, sl st, ch 3, sl st) in corner ch-2 sp, ch 3, sk 2 sc, (sl st, ch 3, sl st) in next sc, ch 2, sk 1 sc, sl st in next sc] in each corner; join with sl st in top of ch-3, fasten off.❀

Welcome the new baby with a cloud-soft coverlet made in classic pink, blue and white. This easy-to-make afghan is the perfect selection for a beginner project.

Soft as a Cloud

By
DELLA BRENNEISE

Skill Level
Easy

Size
33" x 36"

Materials
3-ply sport-weight yarn: 7 oz. pink and blue, 5 oz. white
Hook size I/9 (5.50mm)

Gauge
9 sc rows = 2"; 9 sc = 2½"

Instructions

Row 1: With pink, ch 121, sc in 2nd ch from hook and in each ch across, turn.
Rows 2-10: Ch 1, sc in each sc across, turn. At end of row 10, fasten off pink, turn.
Row 11: Join white in 1st sc, ch 1, sc in same sc, * work elongated dc in sc 2 rows directly below next sc, sc in next sc, repeat from * across, turn.
Row 12: Ch 1, sc in each st across, fasten off white, turn.
Row 13: Join blue with sl st in 1st sc, ch 1, sc in each sc across, turn.
Rows 14-22: Continuing with blue, repeat rows 2-10.
Rows 23-24: With white, repeat rows 11-12.
Continuing in established pattern, work 5 pink stripes and 4 blue stripes with white trim between.

Edging:
Rnd 1: Join white with sl st to upper right corner, ch 1, sc evenly spaced around entire outer edge with 3 sc in each corner, join with sl st in 1st sc.
Rnds 2-6: Ch 1, sc in each sc around with 3 sc in each corner sc, join. At end of rnd 6, fasten off.
Rnd 7: Join blue in any st along edge, (sc in next sc, elongated dc into sc 2 rows below) around, with (elongated dc in corner st 2 rows below, sc in sc, elongated dc in same corner st, sc in sc, elongated dc in same corner st) in each corner, join, fasten off.❁

Super-soft, washable baby yarn in pink and white is the choice for a sugar-and-spice afghan for the new little girl in your life. Choose aqua, mint or yellow for a baby boy.

Candy Ripples

By
ALINE SUPLINSKAS

Skill Level
Easy

Size
38" x 52" including fringe

Materials
Baby yarn: 8¾ oz. pink, 5¼ oz. white
Hook size F/5 (4.00mm)

Gauge
4 dc = 1"; 2 dc rows = 1"

Instructions

Notes:
1. Work entire afghan in back lps only.
2. Ch-3 counts as 1 dc.
3. Dec 1 dc at beginning and end of each row as follows: Yo, draw up lps in each of next 2 sts, yo, draw through 3 lps on hook, yo, draw through 2 remaining lps.

Row 1: With pink, ch 187, sc in 2nd ch from hook and in each of next 3 ch, 3 sc in next ch, sc in next 4 ch, (sk 2 ch, sc in next 4 ch, 3 sc in next ch, sc in next 4 ch) across, turn. (17 points)
Row 2: Ch 3, dec 1 dc, dc in next 2 sts, 3 dc in next st, dc in next 4 sts, (sk 2 sts, dc in next 4 sts, 3 dc in next st, dc in next 4 dc) across to within last 2 sts, dec 1 dc over last 2 sts, turn.
Rows 3-7: Repeat row 2. At end of row 7, fasten off.

Rows 8-13: Join white, repeat row 2, working 2 rows white, 2 rows pink, then 2 rows white. At end of row 13, fasten off white, join pink.
Repeat rows 2-13 5 times. Then repeat rows 2-7 once, turn.
Final row: Ch 1, working through both lps, (sk 2 sts, sc in next 3 sts, sc, ch 1, sc in next st, sc in next 4 sts) across to within last 2 sts, sk 1 st, sc in last st, fasten off.

Fringe:
For each fringe, cut six 8" strands of white; fold strands in half, draw fold through st at bottom of afghan, draw cut ends through fold, pull to secure. Attach fringe in each point and between points at each end of afghan. Trim ends to 3½". ❋

Perennial Garden

From vivid and fanciful flowers to delicate, lace-edged blossoms, fresh and lively floral afghans bring a feeling of spring into any room of your home. Create an heirloom teal and rose afghan you'll cherish forever, or make a soft pastel garden afghan for a special gift. Each design in this collection blooms with just-picked beauty that will last, year after delightful year.

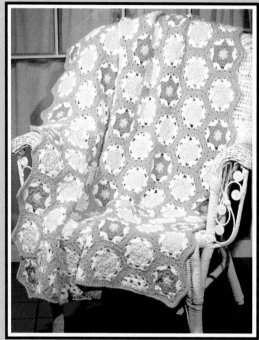

Granny's Favorite

By
KATHERINE ENG

Skill Level
Easy

Size
40" x 58"

Materials
4-ply worsted-weight yarn: 14 oz. green, 10 oz. purple, 8 oz. light green, 3 oz. raspberry, 2 oz. lavender, 2 oz. blue
Hook size F/5 (4.00mm)

Gauge
Center flower = 2½"; 1 square = 6"

Instructions

Center flower (make 18 blocks each with lavender-, raspberry- and blue-center flowers — 54 blocks in all):
Rnd 1: With color, ch 4, join to form ring, ch 1, [sc, ch 3] 7 times in ring, ending with sc, ch 1, hdc in 1st sc.
Rnd 2: Ch 1, (sc, ch 3, sc) in same ch-sp (picot petal made), ch 3, (picot petal in next ch-sp, ch 3) around, join with sl st in 1st sc, fasten off. (8 petals)
Rnd 3: Join purple in ch-3 sp between picot petals, ch 1, picot petal in same ch sp, ch 3, sk next picot petal, (picot petal in next ch-3 sp, ch 3, sk next picot petal) around, join with sl st in 1st sc.
Rnd 4: Sl st into next ch-3 sp, ch 1, picot petal in same sp, ch 1, sc in next ch-sp, ch 1, (picot petal in next ch-sp, ch 1, sc in next ch-sp, ch 1) around, join, fasten off.
Rnd 5: Join green in any ch-3 sp, ch 1, sc in same ch-sp, * ch 2, sk next sc and next ch-1 sp, dc in next sc, ch 2, sk next ch-1 sp and next sc, (2 dc, ch 3, 2 dc) in next ch-3 sp for corner, ch 2, sk next sc and

ch-1 sp, dc in next sc, ch 2, sk next ch-1 sp and next sc, sc in next ch-3 sp, repeat from * around, join.
Rnd 6: Ch 1, sc in each st, 2 sc in each ch-2 sp and (2 sc, ch 2, 2 sc) in each corner ch-3 sp, join, fasten off.
Rnd 7: Join lt. green in 2nd ch to the left of any corner sp, ch, sc in 1st sc, (ch 1, sk next sc, sc in next sc) around, with (ch 1, sk 1 sc, sc, ch 3, sc) in each corner sp, join, fasten off.

Assembly:
Holding blocks right sides together and working through back lps only with lt. green, following diagram, sew blocks together.

Border:
Rnd 1 (right side): Join lt. green in ch-1 sp near center of any block on long side edge of afghan, ch 1, sc in same sp, sc in each sc and in each ch-1 sp, hdc in ch-3

Continued on page 79

This bright and bold afghan is right at home in any decor from traditional to contemporary. Choose your favorite flower color for a custom decorator look.

Formal Gardens

By
CHRISTINA MCNEESE

Skill Level
Average

Size
46" x 65"

Materials
4-ply worsted-weight yarn: 16 oz. each raspberry, spring green and Aran
Hook size H/8 (5.00mm)

Gauge
11 sts = 4"; 5 dc rows = 4"

Instructions

Note: *Each block of graph equals 1 dc.*

Row 1: With spring green, ch 128, dc in 4th ch from hook and following graph, repeat graph 7 times across, turn. (126 dc)

Row 2: Ch 3, dc in each dc across, following graph for color changes.
Repeat rows 1-14 of graph 5 times.

Fringe:
For each fringe, cut five 12" strands of yarn, using one color for each fringe; fold strands in half, draw fold through st at bottom of afghan, draw cut ends through fold, pull to secure. Knot 29 fringes evenly spaced across top and bottom of afghan, alternating colors as shown in photo. Trim ends evenly.❊

COLOR KEY

☒ Spring green
▣ Raspberry
■ Aran

FORMAL GARDENS

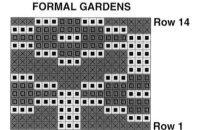

Row 14

Row 1

Repeat pattern across 7 times

Garden Bouquet

By
ROSALIE DEVRIES

Skill Level
Challenging

Size
48" x 68"

Materials
4-ply worsted-weight yarn: 31 oz. raspberry, 20 oz. hot pink, 15 oz. bright green, 14 oz. dark turquoise, 1 oz. maroon
Hook size F/5 (4.00mm)

Gauge
Motif = 6½" square

Instructions

Notes:
1. Popcorn petals rnds will be full but will adjust with completion of next rnd.
2. Post is area between top and bottom of ch.

Rnd 1: With maroon, ch 2, 8 sc in 2nd ch from hook, join with sl st in 1st sc, fasten off.

Rnd 2: Join hot pink in any sc, ch 6, * 3 dc in 5th ch from hook, [remove hook from lp, insert hook through top of 1st ch, pull dropped lp through, pull to tighten (popcorn made)], ** ch 5, 3 dc in top of previous popcorn, repeat from [to] once, repeat from ** once, sc in same sc ***, sc in next sc, ch 5, repeat from * 6 times, repeat from * to *** once, join with sl st in 1st ch of 1st ch-6, fasten off. (8 popcorn petals)

Rnd 3: Join raspberry in any ch-5 post of center popcorn of 3-popcorn petal, ch 6, * 3 dc in 5th ch from hook, repeat from [to] of rnd 2, ** ch 5, 3 dc in top of previous popcorn, repeat from ** once, sc in same ch-5 post ***, ch 5, repeat from * to *** once, ch 1, sc in next center popcorn ch-5 of next popcorn petal, ch 5, repeat from 1st * 6 times, repeat from 1st * to 1st *** 2 times, ch 1, join with sl st in 1st ch of 1st ch-6, fasten off. (16 popcorn petals)

Rnd 4: Join brt. green in any center popcorn ch-5 lp of a 3-popcorn petal of rnd 3, ch 4, 6 tr in same ch-5 post, * [5 sc on next center ch-5 post of next 3-popcorn petal] 3 times, 7 tr on next center ch-5 post of next 3-popcorn petal, repeat from * around, join with sl st in 4th ch of 1st ch-4, fasten off.

Rnd 5 (first motif only): [Join turquoise in 3rd tr of previous rnd, ch 10, hdc in 9th ch from hook, sk next tr, sc in next tr, * ch 5, hdc in 5th ch from hook, sk next tr, sc in next tr, ch 5, dc in 5th ch from hook, sk next 2 sc, sc in next sc, ** ch 5, dc in 5th ch from hook, sk next 4 sc, sc in next sc, repeat from ** once, ch 5, dc in 5th ch from hook, sk next 2 sc, sc in next tr, ch

Continued on page 78

Garden Bouquet

Continued from page 76

5, hdc in 5th ch from hook, sk next tr, sc in next tr], ch 9, hdc in 9th ch from hook, sk next tr, sc in next tr, repeat from * around, join with sl st in 1st ch of 1st ch-10, fasten off.

Note: *All remaining motifs will be joined using following Rnd 5.*

Rnd 5: Repeat from [to] of first motif rnd 5; at this point join 2nd motif to 1st motif as follows: ch 4, sc in center ch of ch-9 lp of 1st motif, ch 4 always counting last sc as ch, hdc in 9th ch from hook, sk next tr, sc in next tr on 2nd motif, * ch 2, sc in center ch of next lp on 1st motif, ch 2, hdc in 5th ch from hook, sk next tr, sc in next tr of 2nd motif, ch 2, sc in center ch of next lp on 2nd motif, ch 2, dc in 5th ch from hook, sk next 2 sc, sc in next sc on 2nd motif, ** ch 2, sc in center ch of next lp on 1st motif, ch 2, dc in 5th ch from hook, sk next 4 sc, sc in next sc on 2nd motif, repeat from ** once, ch 2, sc in center ch of next lp on 1st motif, ch 2, dc in 5th ch from hook, sk next 2 sc, sc in next tr on 2nd motif, ch 2, sc in center ch of next lp on 1st motif, ch 2, hdc in 5th ch from hook, sk next tr, sc in next tr on 2nd motif, ch 4, sc in center ch of next ch-9 lp of 1st motif, ch 4, hdc in 9th ch from hook, sk next tr, sc in next tr of 2nd motif; on motifs with 2 sides and corners joined, repeat from * once, complete 2nd motif as previously instructed.

Border:

Rnd 1: To work narrow edge of afghan, join turquoise in 5th ch of corner ch-9 lp, ch 6, dc in 5th ch from hook, sc in center ch of next lp, [ch 5, dc in 5th ch from hook, sc in center ch of next lp] 5 times, ch 5, dc in 5th ch from hook, sc in center of joining, * repeat from [to] 6 times, ch 5, dc in 5th ch from hook, sc in center of joining, repeat from * 4 times, repeat from [to] 6 times, ch 5, dc in 5th ch from hook, sc in 5th ch of corner ch-9 lp, ** repeat from [to] 6 times, ch 5, dc in 5th ch from hook, sc in center of joining, repeat from ** 8 times, repeat from [to] 6 times, ch 5, dc in 5th ch from hook, sc in 5th ch of corner ch-9 lp, *** repeat from [to] 6 times, ch 5, dc in 5th ch from hook, sc in center of joining, repeat from *** 5 times, repeat from [to] 6 times, ch 5, dc in 5th ch from hook, sc in 5th ch of corner ch-9 lp, **** repeat from [to] 6 times, ch 5, dc in 5th ch from hook, sc in center of joining, repeat from **** 8 times, repeat from [to] 6 times, ch 5, dc in 5th ch from hook, join with sl st in 1st ch of ch-6, turn.

Rnd 2: Sl st to center of last ch-5, ch 6, tr in 5th ch from hook, sc in center ch of next lp, [ch 5, dc in 5th ch from hook, sc in center ch of next lp] 68 times, * ch 5, tr in 5th ch from hook, sc in center ch of next lp, repeat from * once, repeat from [to] 47 times, ** ch 5, tr in 5th ch from hook, sc in center ch of next lp, repeat from ** once, repeat from first [around, join with sl st in 1st ch of ch 6, fasten off.❈

Granny's Favorite

Continued from page 73

sps at corners of blocks and in each joining seam, and (sc, ch 3, sc) in each corner of afghan, join, turn.

Rnd 2: Ch 1, sc in same sc, (ch 1, sk 1 sc, sc in next sc) around, with (ch 1, sk 1 sc, sc, ch 3, sc) in each corner sp, join, fasten off, turn.

Rnd 3: Join green in any ch-1 sp on long side edge, ch 4, sk 1 sc, dc in next sp, (ch 1, sk 1 sc, dc in next ch-1 sp) around, with (ch 1, sk 1 sc, 2 dc, ch 2, 2 dc) in each corner sp, join with sl st in 3rd ch of beginning ch-4.

Rnd 4: Ch 3, dc in next ch-1 sp and in each dc and ch-1 sp around, with (2 dc, ch 2, 2 dc) in each corner sp, join with sl st in top of ch-3, fasten off, turn.

Rnd 5: Join purple in 14th dc to the left of any corner ch-2 sp, ch 1, sc in same st, (ch 2, sk 2 dc, sc in next dc) around, with [ch 2, sk 1 dc, (sc, ch 3, sc) in corner sp, ch 2, sk 1 dc, sc in next dc] in each corner, join with sl st in 1st sc, turn.

Rnd 6: Sl st into 1st ch-sp, ch 1, sc in same sp, (ch 2, sc in next sp) around, with (ch 2, sc, ch 3, sc) in each corner sp, join.

Rnd 7: Sl st into ch-sp, ch 1, sc in 1st sp, * (2 dc, ch 2, 2 dc) in next ch-sp (shell made), sc in next ch-sp, repeat from * around, join, sl st in next dc, turn.

Rnd 8: Ch 1, sc in next sc, * (ch 2, sc, ch 2, sc) in ch-2 sp of shell, ch 2, sc in next sc, repeat from * around, with [ch 3, (sc, ch 3, sc) in corner sp, ch 3, sc in next st] in each corner, join, fasten off, turn.

Rnd 9 (right side): Join raspberry in any sc on long side edge between shell points, ch 1, sc in same sc, * (ch 2, sc, ch 2, sc) in ch-2 sp of next shell, ch 2, sc in next sc between shell points, repeat from * around, with (ch 2, sc, ch 3, sc) in each of 3 ch-3 sps at corners, join, fasten off.❀

COLOR KEY

L Lavender-center flower
R Raspberry-center flower
B Blue-center flower

GRANNY'S FAVORITE
Diagram for Sewing Squares Together

L	B	R	L	B	R
B	R	L	B	R	L
R	L	B	R	L	B
L	B	R	L	B	R
B	R	L	B	R	L
R	L	B	R	L	B
L	B	R	L	B	R
B	R	L	B	R	L
R	L	B	R	L	B

The beauty and color of summer roses are reflected in this soft and comfy afghan. Unique cross stitches and a scalloped border add textural interest.

Rose Trellis

By
DORRIS BROOKS

Skill Level
Average

Size
45" x 70"

Materials
4-ply knitting worsted: 10½ oz. medium rose,
14 oz. pink, 14 oz. dark rose
Hook size I/9 (5.50mm)

Gauge
3 sc = 1"

Instructions

Notes:
1. Cross st (cross stitch): Sk next st, dc in next st, working around dc just made, dc in skipped st.
2. Cl (cluster st): Yo, insert hook in st, yo, draw up a lp, yo, draw through 2 lps on hook, [yo, insert hook in same st, yo, draw up a lp, yo, draw through 2 lps on hook] 2 times, yo, draw through all lps on hook.

Block (make 40):
Rnd 1: With med. rose, ch 4, join to form ring, ch 4, [dc in ring, ch 1] 11 times, join with sl st in 3rd ch of beginning ch-4, fasten off.
Rnd 2: Join pink in any ch-1 sp, ch 3, [yo, draw up a lp, yo, draw through 2 lps on hook] 2 times in same ch-1 sp, yo, draw through all lps on hook (beginning cl made), [ch 2, cl in next ch-1 sp] 11 times, ch 2, join in top of beginning ch-3, fasten off.
Rnd 3: Join dk. rose in any ch-2 sp, ch 3, [2 dc, ch 2, 3 dc] in same sp for corner, * [3 dc in next ch-2 sp] 2 times, [3 dc, ch 2, 3 dc] in next ch-2 sp, repeat from * 2 times, [3 dc in next ch-sp] 2 times, join with sl st in top of beginning ch-3, fasten off.
Rnd 4: Join med. rose in any corner ch-sp, ch 3, [2 dc, ch 2, 3 dc] in same sp, * sk next st, [cross-st] 5 times, sk next st, [3 dc, ch 2, 3 dc] in next corner, repeat from * 2 times, sk next st, [cross-st] 5 times, join in top of ch-3, fasten off.
Rnd 5: Join pink in any corner sp, ch 3, [2 dc, ch 2, 3 dc] in same sp, * sk next st, [cross-st] 6 times, sk next st, [3 dc, ch 2, 3 dc] in next corner, repeat from * 2 times, sk next st, [cross-st] 6 times, join in top of ch-3, fasten off.
Rnd 6: Join dk. rose in any corner sp, ch 1, * [sc, ch 1, sc] in corner sp, sc in each dc across edge, repeat from * around, join, fasten off.

Assembly:
Holding blocks right sides together and working in back lps only, with dk. rose,

Continued on page 87

Brighten a bedroom with an afghan that's as fresh and pretty as flowers in the morning. Hexagonal blocks are made separately and sewn together for a relaxing, portable project.

Pretty Posies

By
SHARON VOLKMAN

Skill Level
Easy

Size
39" x 54"

Materials
4-ply worsted-weight yarn: 21 oz. baby green, 13 oz. white, 10½ oz. pink, 5½ oz. lilac, 3½ oz. pale yellow
Hook size I/9 (5.50mm)

Gauge
1 motif = 5" wide

Instructions

Motif (make 95):
Rnd 1: With pale yellow, ch 4, 11 dc in 4th ch from hook, join, fasten off.
Note: Make 28 motifs with lilac flowers and 67 with pink flowers.
Rnd 2: Join flower color in any dc, ch 3, 2 dc in same st, sc in next st, [3 dc in next st, sc in next st] around, join.
Rnd 3: Sl st in next dc, ch 1, sc in same dc, 5 dc in next sc, [sc in center dc of next group, 5 dc in next sc] around, join, fasten off.
Rnd 4: Join white in any sc, ch 3, 2 dc, ch 2, 3 dc in same st for corner, ch 2, [(3 dc, ch 2, 3 dc) in next sc for corner, ch 2] around, join, fasten off.
Rnd 5: Join baby green in any corner ch-2 sp, ch 3, 2 dc, ch 2, 3 dc in same ch-2 sp, 3 dc in next ch-2 sp on side edge, [(3 dc, ch 2, 3 dc) in next ch-2 corner sp, 3 dc in next ch-2 sp on side edge] around, join, fasten off.

Half-Motif (make 8):
Row 1: With white, ch 4, [3 dc, ch 3, 4 dc] in 4th ch from hook, turn.
Row 2: Ch 3, 3 dc in same st, ch 2, 3 dc in ch-2 sp, ch 2, sk 3 dc, 4 dc in top of beginning ch-3, turn.
Row 3: Ch 3, 3 dc in 1st st, ch 2, [(3 dc, ch 2, 3 dc) in next ch-2 sp, ch 2] 2 times, 4 dc in last st, fasten off white, do not turn.
Row 4: Join baby green in 1st st of row 3, ch 3, 3 dc in same st, 3 dc in next ch-2 sp, [(3 dc, ch 2, 3 dc) in next ch-2 sp, 3 dc in next ch-2 sp] 2 times, 4 dc in last st of row 3, fasten off.

Assembly:
Sew motifs together in 9 strips as follows:
Strip A (make 3): [Lilac motif, pink motif] 5 times, lilac motif.
Strip B (make 4): Half-motif, 10 pink motifs, half-motif.
Strip C (make 2): [Pink motif, lilac motif] 5 times, pink motif.
Sew strips together in the following

Continued on page 87

Spread a tasty summer picnic on this country-style throw! It's easy to make with simple double crochet background, and it's adorned with colorful thread crochet flowers.

Gingham Delight

By
ROSEANNE KROPP

Skill Level
Easy

Size
50" x 60"

Materials
4-ply worsted-weight yarn: 24½ oz. medium blue,
17½ oz. each dark blue and white
Size 10 crochet cotton: 350 yds. each yellow and peach,
300 yds. each dark green and dark red
Hook sizes C/2 (2.50mm) and G/6 (4.50mm),
tapestry needle and yarn needle

Gauge
Worsted-weight yarn: 7 dc = 2"; 7 dc rows = 4"

Instructions

Row 1: With dk. blue and G hook, ch 176, dc in 3rd ch from hook, dc in next 4 ch, to change color, work 4th dc until 2 lps remain on hook, yo with med. blue and complete dc, working over yarn not in use, dc in next 6 ch, changing back to dk. blue in 6th dc, continue across with 6 dc in each color; do not change yarn color on last dc of row, turn. (174)
Note: *Ch 2 does not count as dc. Do not work in turning ch-2.*
Work a total of 3 rows alternating dk. blue with med. blue in same manner. (29 blocks across)
Change to med. blue on last dc of row 3 and fasten off dk. blue. Work next 3 rows alternating 6 med. blue dc with 6 white dc. Continue in pattern, working 3 rows dk. blue and med. blue, then 3 rows med. blue and white, until a length of 35 blocks is completed. Fasten off.

Edging:
Rnd 1: Join white to 1st dc worked on last row, ch 1, sc in same st, sc in each st across, working 2 sc in last dc on row; working in ends of rows down side, 2 sc evenly spaced in end of each row to within last row, 2 sc in corner, sc in each ch across foundation ch, 2 sc in corner, work in ends of rows across remaining edge as before, join. (175 sc on each short side and 211 sc on each long side)
Rnd 2: Sl st in next 4 sc, * sk next 2 sc, 7 sc in next sc, sk next 2 sc, sl st in next sc, repeat from * to within corner sts; to work corner scallop, sk next 2 sts, [5 dc in next sc] twice, sk next 2 sc on next side, sl st in next sc, repeat from * around entire outer edge, join with sl st, fasten off.
Rnd 3: Join dk. blue in 1st dc of 1st scallop, ch 1, sc in same st as ch-1, sc in next 6 dc, [sl st

Continued on next page

Gingham Delight

Continued from page 85

in next sl st, sc in each dc to within sl st] repeat around entire outer edge, join with sl st, fasten off.

Flowers and Leaves:
Note: Wind each ball of crochet cotton into

GINGHAM DELIGHT

two equal balls. Flowers and leaves are worked with 2 strands held together.

Large Flowers (make 12 red and 6 peach):
Rnd 1: With 2 strands yellow size 10 cotton and C hook, ch 4, work 9 dc in 4th ch from hook, drop yellow, with 2 strands flower color, join with sl st in top of beginning ch, fasten off yellow.
Rnd 2: [Ch 4, hdc in 2nd ch from hook, hdc in next 2 chs, sl st in next dc] 10 times; leaving a 10" length of thread, fasten off.

Small Flowers (make 6 red and 12 peach):
Rnd 1: With 2 strands yellow, ch 3, work 8 hdc in 3rd ch from hook, drop yellow, with 2 strands flower color, join with sl st in top of beginning ch, fasten off yellow.
Rnd 2: [Ch 3, hdc in 2nd ch from hook,

hdc in next ch, sl st in next hdc on rnd 1] 9 times; leaving a 10" length of thread, fasten off.

Leaves (make 36):
With 2 strands dk. green, ch 9, dc in 3rd ch from hook, tr in each of next 3 ch, dc in next 2 ch, [sc, ch 2, sc] in last ch; working up opposite side of foundation ch, dc in next 2 ch, tr in next 3 ch, dc in next ch, ch 2, sl st in same ch as last dc; leaving a 10" length of thread, fasten off.

Finishing:
Following diagram, working in backstitch along edge of centers on rnd 1 of flowers and along center foundation ch of leaves, sew flowers and leaves to afghan. Using a pressing cloth, press edging and flowers flat.❀

Rose Trellis

Continued from page 81
sew blocks together in 5 strips of 8 blocks. Sew strips together.

Border:
Rnd 1: Join dk. rose in any corner sp, ch 1, * [sc, ch 1, sc] in corner sp, sc evenly spaced across edge, repeat from * around afghan, join.
Rnd 2: Ch 1, sc in each sc around with [sc, ch 1, sc] in each corner, join, fasten off.
Rnd 3: Join pink in any corner, ch 3, [2 dc, ch 2, 3 dc] in same sp, * sk next st, [cross-st] across edge to within last st before corner, sk next st (it may be necessary to

skip 2 sts here to make pattern come out even), [3 dc, ch 2, 3 dc] in corner sp, repeat from * around, join, fasten off.
Rnds 4-5: Sl st into corner ch-2 sp, ch 3, [2 dc, ch 2, 3 dc] in corner ch-2 sp, * sk next st, [cross-st] across edge to within last st before corner, sk next st, [3 dc, ch 2, 3 dc] in corner, repeat from * around, join with sl st in beginning ch-3. At end of rnd 5, fasten off.
Rnd 6: Join dk. rose in any corner ch-2 sp, ch 1, * [2 sc, ch 2, 2 sc] in corner sp, [sk 2 sts, (2 sc, ch 1, 2 sc) in next st] across to corner, repeat from * around, join, fasten off.❀

Pretty Posies

Continued from page 82
sequence: A, B, C, B, A, B, C, B, A.

Edging:
Join baby green in any corner ch-2 sp, ch 3, [dc, ch 2, 2 dc] in same sp, dc in each st around, working [2 dc, ch 2, 2 dc] in

each outside corner ch-2 sp, 2 dc in side of each row of half-motifs, dc in same ch as beginning dc of half-motifs and working dec in inside corners along edges by working [2 dc together in ch-sp and adjacent dc] twice, sl st to join, fasten off.❀

The quilter's favorite nine-patch pattern gets a sprinkling of cherry pink flowers in this stunning creation. A dainty shell-stitched border adds extra charm.

Floral Nine-Patch

By
KATHERINE ENG

Skill Level
Average

Size
42" x 52"

Materials
4-ply worsted-weight yarn: 24½ oz. bright pink,
21 oz. dark pink, 7 oz. medium avocado
Hook size F/5 (4.00mm)

Gauge
Flowers = 2¾" across; beginning small square = 1¼"

Instructions

Flowers (make 31):
Rnd 1: With dk. pink, ch 4, join with sl st to form ring, ch 1, 8 sc in ring, join.
Rnd 2: Ch 4, retaining last lp of each st on hook, 2 tr in same st as ch-4, yo, draw through all lps on hook, ch 4, sl st in same sc, * ch 2, sl st in next sc, ch 4, retaining last lp on hook, 2 tr in same st as ch-4, yo, draw through all lps on hook, ch 4, sl st in same sc, repeat from * around until 6 petals are completed, ch 2, sk 1 sc, sl st in beginning sc, fasten off.
Leaf #1: Join avocado in any ch-2 sp, ch 6, sc in 2nd ch from hook, sc in next ch, hdc in each of next 2 ch, sc in last ch, sl st in same ch-2 sp, ch 6 behind 2 flower petals, sl st in next ch-2 sp, do not fasten off.
Leaf #2: Ch 5, sc in 2nd ch from hook, sc in next ch, hdc in next ch, sc in next ch, sl st in same ch-2 sp, ch 6 behind 2 flower petals, sl st in next ch-2 sp, do not fasten off.
Leaf #3: Repeat leaf #2, sl st in beginning ch-2 sp, fasten off.

Block 1:
Patch 1:
Row 1 (right side): With dk. pink, ch 6, sc in 2nd ch from hook, (ch 1, sk 1 ch, sc in next ch) 2 times, turn.
Row 2: Ch 1, sc in 1st sc, (ch 1, sk ch-1 sp, sc in next sc) 2 times, turn.
***Note:** Row 2 establishes pattern for remaining patches and squares.*
Rows 3-5: Repeat row 2. At end of row 5, fasten off.
Patch 2:
Row 1 (right side): Join brt. pink in 5th foundation ch of patch 1, ch 14, re- peat row 1 of patch 1 working () 5 more times (7 sc and 6 ch-1 sps), sl st to row 1 of patch 1, sl st up 1 row on patch 1, turn.
Row 2: Repeat row 2 of patch 1.
Row 3: Repeat row 2 of patch 1, sl st to row 3 of patch 1, sl st up 1 row, turn.
Row 4: Repeat row 2 of patch 1.
Row 5: Repeat row 2 of patch 1, sl st to top of patch 1, do not fasten off.

Continued on page 90

Floral Nine-Patch

Continued from page 88

Patch 3:
Work pattern st of row 2 across top of patch 1 for 11 rows, fasten off.

Patch 4:
Join dk. pink to 13th foundation ch of patch 2. Repeat patch 1, sl stitching to side rows of patch 2; at end of row 5, sl st in end sc of patch 2.

Patch 5:
Repeat pattern of row 2 across top of patch 2 for 11 rows, sl stitching to side rows of patch 3. At end of last row, sl st in end sc of patch 3.

Patch 6:
Work pattern of row 2 across top of patch 3 for 5 rows, fasten off.

Patch 7:
Join brt. pink in end sc of patch 4, work pattern st of row 2 across top of patch 4 for 11 rows, sl stitching to side rows of patch 5.

Patch 8:
Work pattern st of row 2 across top of patch 5 for 5 rows, sl stitching to side rows of patch 6, fasten off.

Patch 9:
Join dk. pink and work pattern st of row 2 across top of patch 7 for 5 rows, sl stitching to side rows of patch 8, fasten off.

Block 2:

Row 1: Join brt. pink to 5th foundation ch of patch 4 of block 1, ch 26, work as for row 1 of patch 1, sl st to row 1 of block 1, sl st up to row 2, turn.

Rows 2-21: Work in pattern st, sl stitching to corresponding rows of block 1. At end of row 21, sl st to top sc of block 1.

Block 3:

Work pattern st of row 2 across top of block 1 for 21 rows, fasten off.

Remaining Blocks:

To continue, join and ch to begin another 9-patch block. Complete block, then work 9-patch blocks on tops of plain blocks, working ch 1 over joining seams. Then, join and ch at bottom again to begin plain block; work plain blocks on tops of 9-patch blocks across diagonally. Continue, referring to photo, to complete 32 9-patches and 31 plain blocks.

When working 9-patch blocks after block 1, it is possible to work patches 4, 5 and 6 across in one long diagonal strip if all first 3 patches of each block are first worked on each plain block.

Attaching Flowers:

Upon completion of each plain set of blocks, position and attach flowers. Place flower in center of block so that 2 short leaves face up and cross top left corner (see diagram), and long leaf points toward bottom right corner. Thread yarn needle with 18" of brt. pink, and leaving a 3" length of yarn at back, stitch over scs on rnd 1 of flower and through plain block. Bring yarn to back, tie to short end; weave short end in. Split plies on long length; bring one long length through to front of block and carefully blind-stitch leaves and petals to block.

Border:

Rnd 1: Join avocado in any sc on edge, ch 1, sc evenly spaced around entire outer edge with (sc, ch 2, sc) in each corner, join.

Rnd 2: Ch 1, sc in each sc around with (sc, ch 2, sc) in each corner, join, fasten off.

Note: On rnd 3, in order to make pattern come out even at corners, adjust on top and bottom edge by skipping 3 sc (instead of 2) after shells twice.

Rnd 3: Join dk. pink in 3rd sc to the right of any corner, ch 1, sc in same sc, sk 2 sc, 5 dc in corner ch-2 sp, * sk 2 sc, sc in next sc, sk 2 sc, 5 dc in next sc, repeat from * around with 5 dc in each corner ch-2 sp, join with sl st in 1st sc, turn.

Rnd 4: Sl st to center of next 5-dc group, ch 1, * sc in center dc of 5-dc group, 5 dc in next sc, repeat from * around with (sc in 2nd dc, 5 dc in center dc, dc in 4th dc) in each corner 5-dc group; at end of rnd, join with sl st in 1st sc, turn.

Rnds 5-7: Repeat rnd 4.

Rnd 8: Ch 1, sc in each st around with

(sc, ch 2, sc) in center dc of each corner 5-dc group, join with sl st in 1st sc.
Rnd 9: * Ch 3, sk 3 sc, (sl st, ch 3, sl st) in ch-2 sp, ch 3, sk 3 sc, sl st in next sc, repeat from * around entire edge, join with sl st in 1st ch of ch-3, fasten off.❈

FLORAL NINE-PATCH

Begin patch 1 of bl. 6 here

Bl. 6

Bl. 3

Bl. 5

Begin patch 1 of bl. 5 here

| 6 | 8 | 9 |
| 3 | Bl. 1 5 | 7 |

Bl. 2

Bl. 4

Start here

| 1 | 2 | 4 |

| 1 |

Ch out here to begin bl. 7

Ch out here to begin patch 1 of bl. 4

All patches can be worked across in 1 continuous diagonal.

Special Effects

Add a little sizzle to your decor with one of these dazzling, fun-to-make accents. Designed for maximum visual appeal, these distinctive afghans are sure to become the focal point of any room. Dress up a Southwestern room with a wash of desert color, brighten the den or family room with a stunning plaid, or top off your holiday decorating with cheery red and white stripes.

Designed during Desert Storm, this spectacular gold-fringed afghan pays tribute to the USA. Show your patriotic spirit with a brilliant flash of stars and stripes.

Old Glory

By
LYNN BIGELOW

Skill Level
Easy

Size
45" x 60" plus fringe

Materials
4-ply worsted-weight yarn: 30 oz. white,
24 oz. red, 5 oz. medium gold, 4 oz. blue
Hook sizes G/6 (4.50mm) and I/9 (5.50mm)

Gauge
5 dc = 1½"; 3 dc rows = 1½"

Instructions

Notes:
1. This pattern is worked from top to bottom.
2. When working star section, work over strand not in use.
3. To change color, work complete dc with 1st color, draw lp of new color through lp on hook, pull end of 1st color tightly downward.
4. Crochet hook size I is used only for the foundation ch, and remainder of afghan is worked with hook size G.
5. Ch 3 at beginning of row counts as 1st dc throughout.

Instructions:
Row 1: With I hook and blue, ch 114, drop blue, do not fasten off, continue with red, ch 131, turn, change to G hook, dc in 3rd ch from hook, dc in each red dc, draw up a lp of blue (see Notes), drop red, do not fasten off, dc in each ch across, turn. (244)
Row 2: With blue, ch 3, dc in each blue dc with blue, dc in each red dc with red, turn.

Row 3: With red, ch 3, dc in each red dc with red, 6 dc with blue, (with white, work 2 dc, with blue, work 18 dc) 5 times, ending with 2 white dc and 6 blue dc, turn. (244)
Row 4: With blue, ch 3, 5 dc with blue, (2 white dc, 18 blue dc) 5 times, 2 white dc, 6 blue dc, red dc in each dc across, turn.
Row 5: Ch 3, dc in each red dc with red, 3 blue dc, (8 white dc, 12 blue dc) 5 times, ending with 8 white dc, 3 blue dc, turn.
Row 6: Ch 3, 4 blue dc, (4 white dc, 16 blue dc) 5 times, 5 blue dc, red dc in each red dc across, fasten off red and white from star section, turn.
Row 7: Join white, ch 3, white dc in each red dc across, 4 blue dc, (2 white dc, 2 blue dc, 2 white dc, 6 blue dc, 2 white dc, 6 blue dc) 5 times, 2 white dc, 2 blue dc, 2 white dc, 4 blue dc, turn.
Row 8: Ch 3, 2 blue dc, (2 white dc, 4

Continued on page 108

The man on your gift list will love this hefty checkered afghan. Try it in black, white and red for a bold, contemporary look just right for a college dorm or first apartment.

Checkerboard Stripes

By
ROSALIE DEVRIES

Skill Level
Average

Size
50" x 63"

Materials
4-ply worsted-weight yarn: 25 oz. blue,
14 oz. brown, 13 oz. coral
Hook size F/5 (4.00mm)

Gauge
5 blocks = 3" tall and 3" wide

Instructions

Row 1: With brown, ch 5, dc in 4th ch from hook, dc in next ch, [ch 8, dc in 4th ch from hook, dc in next ch] 31 times, fasten off, turn. (32 columns)

Row 2: Join blue in end ch (next to top of dc) of last column ch-3 lp, * ch 5, dc in 4th ch from hook, dc in next ch, sk next ch of same ch-3 lp, sl st in next ch, dc in next 3 ch below, sl st in end ch of next column ch-3 lp, repeat from * to end, fasten off, turn.

Row 3: Join brown in end ch of last column ch-3 lp, * ch 5, dc in 4th ch from hook, dc in next ch, sk next ch of same ch-3 lp, sl st in next ch, dc in next 3 dc below, sl st in end ch of next column ch-3 lp, repeat from * across, fasten off, turn.

Row 4: With blue, repeat row 3.

Rows 5-6: Repeat rows 3-4.

Row 7: With coral, repeat row 3.

Row 8: With blue, repeat row 3.

Rows 9-12: Repeat rows 7-8.

Row 13: With brown, repeat row 3.

Row 14: With blue, repeat row 3.

Rows 15-100: Repeat rows 3-14 7 times, then repeat rows 3-4.

Row 101: Join brown in end ch of last column ch-3 lp, ch 1, sl st in same ch, sl st in next 2 ch, * dc in next 3 dc below, sl st in each ch of next column ch-3 lp, repeat from * across, fasten off.

Border:

Rnd 1: Join blue in last sl st of row 101, ch 1, 3 sc in sl st, sc in each sl st and dc to last sl st, 3 sc in last sl st, sc in each dc on edge to last dc, 3 sc in last dc, sc in center and top of same dc, * sc in each of next 3 dc bottoms, 3 sc in side of next dc, repeat from * to last dc, 2 sc in side of last dc, 3 sc in top of last dc, sc in each dc across remaining edge, join with sl st in 1st sc, fasten off, turn.

Rnd 2: Join coral in any back lp of rnd 1, sl st in each back lp around, join with sl st in 1st sl st, fasten off.❈

Shades of the scenic Southwest are displayed in this striking afghan. This desert beauty has a bonus feature — no loose ends! Yarn at beginning and end of each row becomes fringe.

Turquoise Hills

By
MARILYN AGUILAR

Skill Level
Easy

Size
38" x 75"

Materials
4-ply worsted-weight yarn: 21 oz. black, 7 oz. each
rust, peach, light peach and apricot,
3½ oz. turquoise, 2 oz. each light apricot and yellow
Hook size H/8 (5.00mm)

Gauge
7 dc = 2"; [1 dc and 1 sc row] 3 times = 2"

Instructions

Notes:
1. *Afghan is worked on right side only.*
2. *Fasten off at end of each row, leaving a 7" length.*
3. *Leave a 7" length to begin each row.*
4. *For sc rows, ch 1 at beginning of each row and ch-1 does not count as first sc. For dc rows, ch 3 at beginning of each row and ch-3 DOES count as first dc.*

Foundation ch: With black, leaving a 7" length, ch 252; leaving a 7" length, fasten off.
Rows 1-3: With black, sc in each st across.
Row 4: With rust, dc in each st across.
Row 5: With rust, sc in each st across.
Rows 6-7: With peach, repeat rows 4-5.
Rows 8-9: With light peach, repeat rows 4-5.
Rows 10-11: With apricot, repeat rows 4-5.
Row 12: With black, dc in next 5 sts, [long

dc through 2 rows below, dc in next 4 sts] across, ending with dc in final 6 sts. (252)
Rows 13-14: With black, repeat rows 4-5.
Row 15: With black, sc in 3 sc, [with lt. apricot, sc in 3 sc, with black, sc in 3 sc] across.
Row 16: With black, sc in 2 sc, with lt. apricot, sc in 3 sc, [with black, sc in 3 sc, with lt. apricot, sc in 3 sc] across, ending with 4 sc with black.
Row 17: With black, sc in 1 sc, with lt. apricot, sc in 3 sc, repeat [] of row 16 across, ending with 5 sc with black.
Row 18: With black, sc in each sc across.
Rows 19-20: With black, dc in each st across.
Row 21: Repeat row 11.
Row 22: Repeat row 10.
Row 23: Repeat row 9.
Row 24: Repeat row 8.
Row 25: Repeat row 7.
Row 26: Repeat row 6.

Continued on page 109

A deceptively simple stitch pattern forms the basis for this colorful and whimsical striped throw. Made in crayon colors, it's a warm and cozy comfort for a child's naptime.

Nifty Neckties

By
AGNES RUSSELL

Skill Level
Easy

Size
29" x 42"

Materials
4-ply worsted-weight yarn: 8 oz. black, 3½ oz. each bright red, green and purple, 1¾ oz. each yellow and blue
Hook size F/5 (4.00mm)

Gauge
7 sc = 1½"; 7 sc rows in back lps only = 1½"

Instructions

Necktie strips (make 8 — 2 each green, red and purple, and 1 each blue and yellow):
Row 1: With strip color, ch 14, 2 sc in 2nd ch from hook, sc in each of next 4 ch, draw up a lp in next ch, sk next ch, draw up a lp in next ch, yo, draw through all 3 lps on hook, sc in next 4 ch, 2 sc in next ch, turn. (13 sc)
Row 2: Ch 1, working in back lps only, 2 sc in 1st sc, sc in next 4 sc, draw up a lp in next st, sk 1 st, draw up a lp in next st, yo, draw through all 3 lps on hook, sc in next 4 sc, 2 sc in next sc, turn.
Rows 3-120: Repeat row 2.
At end of row 120, fasten off.

First Strip Trim:
Rnd 1: Join black in foundation ch at center bottom point, ch 1, sc in same sp, (ch 3, sk 2 ch, sc in next ch) 2 times, ch 3, sc in side edge of row 1, (ch 3, sk 1 row, sc in end of next row) along edge, ch 3, sc in 1st sc of last row, ch 3, sk 2 sc, sc in next sc, ch 3, sk 7 sc, sc in next sc, ch 3, sk 2 sc, sc in last sc, (ch 3, sk 1 row, sc in end of next row) along edge; working across foundation ch, ch 3, sc in 1st ch, ch 3, sk 2 ch, sc in next sc, ch 3, sl st to join in starting sc, do not turn.
Rnd 2: Ch 1, (sc, ch 3, sc) in next ch-3 lp around, join with sl st in 1st sc, fasten off.

Second Strip Trim:
Rnd 1: Repeat rnd 1 of 1st strip trim.
Rnd 2: Ch 1, (sc, ch 3, sc in next ch-3 lp) across bottom, up side to top, (sc, ch 3, sc in next ch-3 lp) 3 times across top, holdng 1st strip to side edge of 2nd strip and matching ch-3 lps, * sc in next ch-3 lp, ch 1, sl st in matching ch-3 lp of 1st strip, ch 1, sc in same ch-3 lp as last sc on 2nd strip, repeat from * along edge to within last 2 ch-3 lps, (sc, ch 3, sc in next ch-3 lp) 2 times, join, fasten off.
Repeat until all strips are joined.

Continued on page 108

Create the look of traditional plaid with an easy base mesh and chain-stitched vertical stripes. This warm throw brings a note of casual comfort to a den or family room.

Plaid With Pizazz

By
CHRISTINA MCNEESE

Skill Level
Average

Size
54" x 64" plus fringe

Materials
4-ply worsted-weight yarn: 21 oz. yellow, 14 oz. each
federal blue, light federal blue, forest green and sage green
Hook size H/8 (5.00mm)

Gauge
8 squares and 5 rows = 4"

Instructions

Note: *To change colors, in last step of last dc with 1st color, yo with new color, draw through remaining 2 lps on hook, continue with new color.*

Row 1: With forest green, ch 203, dc in 7th ch from hook, (ch 1, sk 1 ch, dc in next ch) across, turn.
Row 2: Ch 3, dc in next dc, (ch 1, sk ch-1 sp, dc in next dc) across, turn.
Rows 3-100: Repeat row 2, working 3 rows forest green, 2 rows sage green, 1 row yellow, 3 rows federal blue, 2 rows light federal blue, 1 row yellow, 1 row federal blue, 2 rows light federal blue and 1 row yellow for a total of 20 pattern rows repeated 5 times. At end of row 100, fasten off.

Vertical Stripes
Notes:
1. Vertical rows are crocheted onto mesh background on right side of afghan.
2. Vertical stripes are worked in the same color and row sequence as mesh background — 20 pattern rows repeated 4 times, with the last repeat having 18 pattern rows.
Row 1: Draw up a lp around opposite side of foundation ch of first square (ch-1 sp), * ch 3, remove hook from lp, insert hook in ch-1 sp of next row, pick up dropped lp and draw through lp on hook, repeat from * to end of row 100, fasten off. Weave in loose ends. Repeat row 1 across afghan.

Fringe:
For each fringe, cut three 15" strands of yellow; fold strands in half, draw fold through st at bottom of afghan, draw cut ends through fold, pull to secure. Knot fringe in every other stitch across top and bottom of afghan. Trim ends evenly.❀

Delicate chain stitches form the beautiful relief pattern on this unique, show-stopping afghan. Create this beauty in glorious shades of your favorite color.

Chains of Beauty

By
RAYMOND E. FARISH

Skill Level
Average

Size
49" x 91"

Materials
4-ply worsted-weight yarn: 41 oz. burgundy,
19 oz. rose, 17 oz. each red and soft pink
Hook sizes K/10½ (6.50mm) and F/5 (4.00mm)

Gauge
3 sc = 1"; 7 rows sc = 2"

Instructions

Note: *Join motifs in the following order:*
1st row: *(Soft pink, rose, red) 4 times.*
2nd row: *Half-motif, (red, soft pink, rose) 3 times, red, soft pink, half-motif.*
Make motifs in order of assembly, and alternate 1st and 2nd rows for a total of 25 rows. Afghan length may be shortened if desired.

Motif #1:
Rnd 1: With K hook and pink, ch 5, sl st in 1st ch to form ring, ch 1, 18 sc in ring, join with sl st in 1st sc (18 sc).
Rnd 2: *(Ch 11, sl st in next sc) twice, ch 5, sl st in next sc, repeat from * 5 times more, sl st in 1st st, fasten off. (6 groups of 2 large and 1 small lps)

Motif #2 (make 99 pink, 100 red, 88 rose):
Rnd 1: Repeat rnd 1 of Motif #1.
Rnd 2: *(Ch 5, sc in center of big lp of adjoining motif, ch 5, sl st in next sc) twice, ch 5, sl st in next sc, repeat from *

to join additional motifs or complete as rnd 2 of 1st motif. Fasten off.

Half-Motif (make 24 rose):
Rnd 1: With rose, repeat rnd 1 of Motif #1.
Rnd 2: *Ch 5, sl st in next sc, (ch 5, sc in center of big lp of adjoining motif, ch 5, sl st in next sc) twice, repeat from * twice more, ch 5, sl st in next sc, fasten off, leaving remaining sc unused.

Small Motif (make 552 burgundy):
Rnd 1: With F hook, ch 2, 6 sc in 2nd ch from hook, join with sl st in 1st sc.
Rnd 2: (Ch 5, sc in small lp of next large motif, ch 5, sl st in next sc, ch 5, sc in same small lp of large motif, ch 5, sl st in next sc) 3 times, join with sl st in 1st st, fasten off.

Border:
Rnd 1: With right side facing and K hook,

Continued on page 109

Add this radiant accent to your holiday decor and enjoy the compliments. Or make it in your favorite team colors for chilly nights at the stadium.

Cheery Cables

By
SANDY HYZAK

Skill Level
Average

Size
44" x 59"

Materials
4-ply worsted-weight yarn: 40 oz. red, 16 oz. white
Hook size H/8 (5.00mm)

Gauge
4 dc = 1"; 6 dc rows = 3"

Instructions

Note: *Ch 3 at beginning of row does not count as 1st dc.*

Row 1: With white, ch 182, dc in 4th ch from hook, dc in each remaining ch across, turn.
Row 2: Ch 3, (fpdc around each of next 4 sts, bpdc around each of next 8 sts, fpdc around each of next 4 sts, dc in next 2 sts) across, ending with dc in last dc, turn.
Row 3: Ch 3, (bpdc around each of next 4 sts, dc in next 8 sts, bpdc around each of next 4 sts, dc in next 2 sts) across, ending with dc in last dc, turn.
Row 4: Ch 3, (fpdc around each of next 4 sts, dc in next 8 sts, fpdc around each of next 4 sts, dc in next 2 sts) across, ending with dc in last dc, turn.
Rows 5-6: Repeat rows 3-4.
Row 7: Ch 3, (bpdc around next 16 sts, dc in next 2 sts) across, fasten off white, turn.
Rows 8-10: With red, repeat rows 2-4.
Rows 11-12: Repeat rows 3-4.
Row 13: Repeat row 7.

Rows 14-19: With white, repeat rows 8-13.
Rows 20-25: With red, repeat rows 8-13.
Rows 26-31: With white, repeat rows 8-13.
Rows 32-103: With red, repeat rows 8-13.
Rows 104-109: With white, repeat rows 8-13.
Rows 110-115: With red, repeat rows 8-13.
Rows 116-121: With white, repeat rows 8-13.
Rows 122-127: With red, repeat rows 8-13.
Rows 128-133: With white, repeat rows 8-13.
Row 134: With white, repeat row 2, fasten off.

Edging:
Rnd 1: Join red in same st and working down side, ch 3, dc in row end, 2 dc in each row end, 3 dc in corner, dc in each st across bottom, 3 dc in corner, 2 dc in each row end, 3 dc in corner, dc in each st across top, join.
Rnd 2: Ch 3, dc in each dc around, with 3 dc in each corner st, join, fasten off.❈

Old Glory

Continued from page 95

blue dc, 2 white dc, 5 blue dc, 2 white dc, 5 blue dc) 5 times, 2 white dc, 4 blue dc, 2 white dc, 3 blue dc, white dc in each white dc across, turn.

Row 9: Ch 3, dc in each white dc across, 13 blue dc, (8 white dc, 12 blue dc) 4 times, 8 white dc, 13 blue dc, turn.

Row 10: Ch 3, 14 blue dc, (4 white dc, 16 blue dc) 4 times, 4 white dc, 15 blue dc, white dc in each white dc across, turn.

Row 11: Ch 3, dc in each white dc, 6 blue dc, (2 white dc, 6 blue dc, 2 white dc, 2 blue dc, 2 white dc, 6 blue dc) 5 times, 2 white dc, 6 blue dc, turn.

Row 12: Ch 3, 5 blue dc, (2 white dc, 5 blue dc, 2 white dc, 4 blue dc, 2 white dc, 5 blue dc) 5 times, 2 white dc, 6 blue dc, white dc in each white dc across, fasten off white, turn.

Note: On rows 13-36, work stripe pattern of (6 rows red, 6 rows white) twice. Pattern repeats indicated are for star section only.

Rows 13-36: Repeat rows 5-12 for star pattern, working stripe pattern as indicated in previous Note.

Rows 37-42: Repeat rows 5-10 for star pattern, working 6 rows stripe pattern with red.

Rows 43-48: With white, ch 3, dc in each dc across, turn. (244)

At end of row 48, fasten off white, turn.

Rows 49-78: Repeat row 43, alternating 6 rows each of red and white, ending with red.

At end of row 78, fasten off.

Fringe:
Fringe is worked around entire outer edge of afghan. On opposite side of foundation ch and row 78, attach fringe in every 3rd st; on side edges, attach fringe in end of each row.

For each fringe, cut five 10" strands of gold; fold strands in half, draw fold through st at bottom of afghan, draw cut ends through fold, pull to secure. When all fringe is complete, trim ends evenly.❈

Nifty Neckties

Continued from page 101

Afghan trim:
Rnd 1: Join black in any ch-3 lp, ch 1, (sc, ch 1, sc) in same ch-3 lp, (sc, ch 3, sc) in next ch-3 lp around entire edge of afghan, with (sc, ch 3, sc) in center of each joining section, join with sl st, fasten off.

Fringe:
For each fringe, cut four 12" strands of yarn; fold strands in half, draw fold through ch-3 lp at bottom of afghan, draw cut ends through fold, pull to secure. Mixing colors as shown in photo, fringe in each ch-3 lp across top and bottom.❈

Turquoise Hills

Continued from page 98

Row 27: Repeat row 5.
Row 28: Repeat row 4.
Rows 29-37: Repeat rows 12-20 with yellow instead of lt. apricot.
Rows 38-45: Repeat rows 4-11.
Rows 46-47: With black, repeat rows 4-5.
Row 48: With turquoise, sc in each st across.
Row 49: With black, sc in each st across.
Row 50: With black, dc in 6 sts, with turquoise, dc in 20 sts, [with black, dc in 2 sts, with turquoise, dc in 20 sts] 10 times, ending with dc in 6 sts with black.
Row 51: With black, dc in 8 sts, with turquoise, dc in 16 sts, [with black, dc in 6 sts, with turquoise, dc in 16 sts] 10 times, ending with dc in 8 sts with black.
Row 52: With black, dc in 10 sts, with turquoise, dc in 12 sts, [with black, dc in 10 sts, with turquoise, dc in 12 sts] 10 times, ending with dc in 10 sts with black.
Row 53: With black, dc in 12 sts, with turquoise, dc in 8 sts, [with black, dc in 14 sts, with turquoise, dc in 8 sts] 10 times, ending with dc in 12 sts with black.
Row 54: With black, dc in 14 sts, with turquoise, dc in 4 sts, [with black, dc in 18 sts, with turquoise, dc in 4 sts] 10 times, ending with dc in 14 sts with black.
Row 55: With black, dc in 15 sts, with turquoise, dc in 2 sts, [with black, dc in 20 sts, with turquoise, dc in 2 sts] 10 times, ending with dc in 15 sts with black. (252)
Rows 56-57: With black, repeat rows 4-5.
Row 58: With turquoise, sc in each st across.
Row 59: With black, sc in each st across.
Row 60: [With black, sc in next 2 sts, with turquoise, sc in next 2 sts] across.
First half of afghan is complete.
Starting with row 59 and working back to and including row 1, work second half of afghan.

Fringe:
7" lengths are part of fringe. For remainder of fringe, cut 15" lengths of matching colors; fold strands in half, draw fold through st at bottom of afghan, draw cut ends through fold, pull to secure. Add fringe at end of each row as shown in photo.❁

Chains of Beauty

Continued from page 105

join burgundy with sc in 1st ch-11 lp on bottom left corner, ch 1, sc in next ch-11 lp, ch 1, hdc in next ch-5 lp, ch 1, sc in next ch-11 lp, (*ch 1, sc in next ch-11 lp, ch 1, hdc in next ch-5 lp, [ch 1, sc in next ch-11 lp] twice *, ch 1, dc in next ch-5 lp, {ch 2, tr in middle ch in outside edge of next ch-11, ch 2, tr in joining, ch 2, tr in middle ch in outside edge of next ch-11, ch 2, dc in next ch-5 lp}, ch 1, sc in next ch-11 lp), repeat from (to) across bottom, repeat from * to *, ch 1, hdc in next ch-5 lp, ch 1, sc in next ch-11 lp, (ch 1, dc in next ch-5 lp, repeat from { to }, ch 1, sc in each of next 7 sts) across side, ch 1, dc in next ch-5 lp, repeat from [to], ch 1, sc in next ch-11 lp, repeat across top same as bottom and 2nd long side as 1st long side, join with sl st in 1st sc.
Rnd 2: Sc in each st around, join with sl st in 1st sc.
Rnd 3: Ch 1, (sc in next 26 sts, [*sl st in same sc as last sc, turn, ch 2, sk sl st and next 4 sc, (tr, ch 2) 5 times in next sc, sk next 4 sc, sc in next sc, turn, (sc, ch 3, sc) in each ch-2 sp *, dc in next 3 sc, hdc in next 3 sc, sc in next 3 sc, hdc in next 3 sc, dc in next 3 sc, sc in next 9 sc] 10 times, repeat from * to *, sc in next 30 sc, repeat from * to *, [hdc in next 4 sc, sc in next 9 sc, repeat from * to *, hdc in next 3 sc, sc in next 3 sc, hdc in next 3 sc, repeat from * to *] 12 times) 2 times, join, fasten off.❁

Country Treasures

Country decorating remains a favorite after years of popularity. Warm heirloom furniture, treasured keepsakes and handmade quilts and afghans give rooms a welcoming and relaxing feeling, and are wonderful to return to after each day of our busy lives. Created in the colors of country barns, hand-thrown pottery, freshly turned earth and fragrant wildflowers, these afghans exude country charm.

Reminiscent of golden wheat, furrowed fields and verdant pastures, this homey afghan features several patterned stitches for the beginning crocheter.

Virginia's Reel

By
SISTER VIRGINIA GRAF

Skill Level
Average

Size
52" x 76"

Materials
4-ply worsted-weight yarn: 24 oz. each terra cotta and dark brown, 20 oz. bone, 16 oz. medium gold
Hook size H/8 (5.00mm)

Gauge
3 dc = 1"; 2 rows dc = 1"

Instructions

Note: *It may be necessary to adjust number of stitches by 1 or 2 as needed for pattern repeats.*

Row 1: With med. gold, ch 180, sc in 2nd ch from hook, (ch 1, sk next ch, sc in next ch) across, turn. (179)
Row 2: Ch 1, sc in 1st sc, (dc in ch-1 sp, sc in next sc) across, turn.
Row 3: Ch 1, sc in 1st sc, (ch 1, sk next dc, sc in next sc) across, turn.
Rows 4-28: Repeat rows 2-3; end with row 2 and fasten off.
Row 29: Join bone, ch 1, sc in same st and in each sc across, turn.
Row 30: Ch 3, dc in next 8 sts, ch 2, sk 2 sts, (dc in next 3 sts, ch 2, sk 2 sts) across, ending with dc in last 9 sts, turn.
Row 31: Ch 3, dc in next 8 dc, ch 2, dc in next dc, (ch 2, sk 1 dc, dc in next dc, dc in ch-2 sp, dc in next dc) across, ending with ch 2, dc in last 9 sts, turn.
Row 32: Ch 3, dc in next 8 dc, ch 2, (dc in next dc, 2 dc in ch-2 sp, dc in next dc, ch 2, sk 2 sts) across, ending with ch 2, dc in last 9 sts, turn.
Row 33: Ch 3, dc in next 8 sts, ch 2, dc in next dc, (ch 2, sk 2 sts, dc in next dc, 2 dc in ch-2 sp, dc in next dc) across, turn.
Rows 34-35: Repeat rows 32-33.
Row 36: Repeat row 32.
Row 37: Ch 1, sc in each dc, sc in each ch-2 sp across, fasten off, turn.
Row 38: Join terra cotta, ch 3, dc in each st across, turn.
Row 39: Ch 2, fpdc around each of next 4 dc, (bp around next 4 dc, fpdc around next 4 dc) across to last dc, hdc in top of turning ch, turn.
Rows 40-59: Repeat row 39. At end of row 59, fasten off, turn.
Rows 60-68: Join bone, repeat rows 29-37.
Row 69: Join dk. brown, ch 1, sc in each st across, turn.
Row 70: Ch 2, hdc in each st across, turn.

Continued on page 121

A rainbow of scrap yarn colors makes this classic afghan a delight during the holidays or any time of the year. Multicolored blocks are bordered with two shades of gold and black.

Starburst Magic

By
PEARLE GOODWIN

Skill Level
Average

Size
43" x 57"; block size 8" square

Materials
4-ply worsted-weight yarn: 17 oz. black,
15 oz. pale green, 10 oz. each medium gold and light
gold, 8 oz. white, 2 oz. each assorted bright colors
Hook size K10½ (7.00mm)

Gauge
5 sts = 1½"

Instructions

Notes:
1. Make a total of 35 blocks.
2. Make 12 blocks with white for rnd 2, black for rnd 3 and light gold for center and rnd 6 (A blocks).
3. Make 6 blocks with black for rnd 2, white for rnd 3 and lt. gold for center and rnd 6 (B blocks).
4. Make 9 blocks with white for rnd 2, black for rnd 3 and med. gold for center and rnd 6 (C blocks).
5. Make 8 blocks with black for rnd 2, white for rnd 3 and med. gold for center and rnd 6 (D blocks).

Block:
Rnd 1: With center color, ch 4, join to form ring, ch 3, 2 dc in ring, ch 3, (3 dc in ring, ch 3) 3 times, join with sl st in top of ch-3, fasten off.
Rnd 2: Join rnd 2 color in any ch-3 sp, ch 3, (2 dc, ch 3, 3 dc) in same sp, ch 1, * (3 dc, ch 3, 3 dc) in next ch-3 sp, ch 1,

repeat from * around, join, fasten off.
Rnd 3: Join rnd 3 color in any ch-3 sp, ch 3, (2 dc, ch 3, 2 dc) in same sp, * sk 1 dc, dc in next 2 dc, long tr around fp of middle dc in rnd 1 as follows: [yo twice, insert hook from front to back to front around post of dc, (yo, draw through 2 lps on hook) 3 times], sk 1 dc, dc in next 2 dc, (3 dc, ch 3, 3 dc) in next ch-3 sp, repeat from * around, sl st to join, fasten off.
Rnd 4: Join bright color in any ch-3 sp, ch 4, (2 tr, ch 3, 2 tr) in same sp, * sk 1 dc, tr in each of next 2 dc, long tr around fp of next 5 sts, sk 1 dc, tr in next 2 dc, (3 tr, ch 3, 3 tr) in ch-3 sp, repeat from * around, join with sl st, fasten off.
Rnd 5: Join pale green in any ch-3 sp, ch 1, * (3 sc, ch 3, 3 sc) in ch-3 sp, sk 1 st, sc in each of next 4 sts, dc in each of next 6 sts, sc in each of next 4 sts, repeat from * around, join, fasten off.
Rnd 6: Join rnd 6 color in any ch-3 sp, ch

Continued on page 121

You'll love this feminine afghan created with sport-weight yarn and a delightfully airy pattern. It's just right for spring decorating in a bedroom or sun porch.

Apricot Fizz

By
ALINE SUPLINSKAS

Skill Level
Easy

Size
47" x 66"

Materials
3-ply sport-weight yarn: 33 oz. apricot
Hook size G/6 (4.50mm)

Gauge
4 dc = 1"; 3 pattern rows = 1"

Instructions

Row 1 (right side): Ch 197, dc in 4th ch from hook and in each ch across, turn. (195)
Row 2: Ch 1, sk 1 st, (dc in next st, sl st in next st) across, ending with sl st in top of ch-3, turn.
Row 3: Ch 3, (dc in next dc, dc in next sl st) across, ending with last dc in top of ch-3, turn.
Repeat rows 2-3 until afghan is 66" long; end with row 3. Turn.

Trim:
Row 1: Ch 1, sc in 1st st, (ch 3, sk 3 sts, sc in next st) across to within last 3 sts, ch 2, sc in last st, fasten off.
Join in opposite side of foundation ch, repeat row 1 of trim.

Fringe:
For each fringe, cut six 9" strands of yarn; fold strands in half, draw fold through st at bottom of afghan, draw cut ends through fold, pull to secure. Attach fringe in each ch-lp on each end of afghan. Trim ends evenly.❀

The traditional red, white and green of Christmas create a wonderful afghan that brings country cheer to your home all year around. It's extra-warm and reversible, too.

Christmas Stars

By
CHRISTINA MCNEESE

Skill Level
Intermediate

Size
44" x 68" plus fringe

Materials
4-ply worsted-weight yarn: 32 oz. white,
16 oz. each red and green
Hook size G/6 (4.50mm)

Gauge
9 sc = 3"; 7 sc rows = 3"

Instructions

Note: *Work over yarn strands not in use at all times.*

Row 1: With white, ch 128, sc in 2nd ch from hook and in each remaining ch across, turn.
Rows 2-37: Ch 1 at beginning of each row, following graph and changing colors accordingly, sc in each st across, turn each row.
Rows 38-145: Repeat rows 2-37 3 times.

Rows 146-163: Repeat rows 2-19. At end of row 163, fasten off.

Fringe:
For each fringe, cut eight 15" strands of yarn; fold strands in half, draw fold through st at bottom of afghan, draw cut ends through fold, pull to secure. Attach 15 fringes along each end of afghan, alternating colors as shown in photo. Trim ends evenly.❈

Graph on page 120

Christmas Stars

Instructions on page 118

COLOR KEY	
☐	White
⬤	Holly red
◼	Grass green

CHRISTMAS STARS

Virginia's Reel

Continued from page 112

Row 71: Ch 2, sk 1st hdc, (sk next hdc, hdc in next hdc, sc loosely in skipped hdc) across, ending with hdc in top of turning ch, turn.

Row 72: Ch 2, sk 1st hdc, hdc in each st across, end with hdc in top of turning ch, turn.

Rows 73-88: Repeat rows 71-72.

Row 89: Ch 1, sc in each st across, fasten off, turn.

Rows 90-104: Join bone, repeat rows 29-36, then rows 31-37.

Rows 105-125: Join dk. brown, repeat rows 69-89.

Rows 126-134: Join bone, repeat rows 29-37.

Rows 135-156: Join terra cotta, repeat rows 38-59.

Rows 157-165: Join bone, repeat rows 29-37.

Rows 166-193: Join med. gold, repeat rows 1-28.

Border:
Working 3 sc in each corner on each rnd, work 3 rnds sc around entire outer edge with dk. brown; work 3 rnds sc with bone, and 3 rnds sc with terra cotta.❀

Starburst Magic

Continued from page 114

3, (2 dc, ch 3, 3 dc) in same sp, * sk 1 st, dc in next 19 sts, (3 dc, ch 3, 3 dc) in next ch-3 sp, repeat from * around, join, fasten off.

Rnd 7: Join black in any ch-3 sp, ch 1, * (3 sc, ch 2, 3 sc) in ch-3 sp, sk 1 st, sc in next 24 sts, repeat from * around, fasten off.

Assembly:
Holding blocks right sides together, with black, whipstitch blocks together in the following order: Three strips as follows: A, C, A, C, A, C, A. Two strips as follows: D, B, D, B, D, B, D. Whipstitch strips together to form afghan with A block in each corner.

Border:
Rnd 1: Join med. gold in corner of afghan, ch 1, (3 sc, ch 3, 3 sc) in corner, sc in each st and in each joining seam around, with (3 sc, ch 3, 3 sc) in each corner, join with sl st, fasten off.

Rnd 2: Join red or any bright color in corner, ch 3, (2 dc, ch 3, 3 dc) in corner, dc in each st around, with (3 dc, ch 3, 3 dc) in each corner, join, fasten off.

Rnd 3: Join black in corner, ch 3, (2 dc, ch 3, 3 dc) in corner, * sk 1 st, (dc, ch 1, dc) in next st, repeat from * around with (3 dc, ch 3, 3 dc) in each corner, join, fasten off.❀

Made in the favorite country colors of sky blue, barn red and pottery tan, this afghan is large enough to cover a twin-size bed. Extra motifs may be added as desired for larger beds.

Rustic Colors

By
CAROLYN CHRISTMAS

Skill Level
Easy

Size
48" x 72"

Materials
4-ply worsted-weight yarn: 24½ oz. red,
21 oz. each pale blue and beige
Hook size K/10½ (7.00mm)

Gauge
3 rnds = 2"; 7 dc = 2"

Instructions

Big Block (make 70):
Rnd 1: With red, ch 4, join with sl st to form ring, ch 3, 15 dc in ring, join with sl st in top of ch-3. (16)
Rnd 2: Ch 3, dc in same st, 2 dc in each dc around, join, fasten off. (32)
Rnd 3: Join blue with sl st in any dc, ch 3, dc in next 3 dc, ch 3, (dc in next 4 dc, ch 3) around, join, fasten off.
Rnd 4: Join beige with sl st in any ch-3 sp, ch 3, (dc, ch 1, 2 dc) in same sp, dc in next 4 dc, * (2 dc, ch 1, 2 dc) in next ch-3 sp, dc in next 4 dc, repeat from * around, join, fasten off.

Small Block (make 54):
Rnd 1: With blue, repeat rnd 1 of big block, fasten off.
Rnd 2: Join red with sl st in any dc, ch 3, dc in same sp, (2 dc in next st) 3 times, ch 1, (2 dc in each of next 4 sts, ch 1) around, join, fasten off.

Assembly:
Holding blocks wrong sides together and sewing through back lps only, with beige, sew big blocks in 10 strips of 7 blocks each; sew strips together. Sew small blocks diagonally in openings as shown in photo.

Border:
Rnd 1: Join red in corner of any block, ch 1, 3 sc in same sp, sc in each st around, with 3 sc in each corner sp and decrease where blocks join as follows: draw up a lp in last ch-1 sp of 1st block, draw up a lp in 1st ch-1 sp of 2nd block, yo, draw through all lps on hook, join with sl st in 1st sc.
Rnd 2: Ch 1, sc in same st, 2 sc in next st, sc around edge, with 2 sc in each center corner st and dec at joinings as follows: draw up a lp in st before dec on rnd 1, draw up a lp in st after dec on rnd 1, yo, draw through all lps on hook, join with sl st, fasten off.❀

The ever-popular granny square takes on a brilliant twist in this dazzling design. Raised post stitches bring interesting dimension and contrast to the open-weave background.

Crayon Blocks

By
BRENDA LEWIS

Skill Level
Average

Size
42" x 54"

Materials
4-ply worsted-weight yarn: 24½ oz. royal blue,
7 oz. each red, bright green and gold
Hook size I/9 (5.50mm)

Gauge
(3 dc, ch 3) 3 times and 6 pattern rnds = 4"

Instructions

Notes:
1. Fptr (front post treble): Yo twice, insert hook from front to back to front around post of st below, draw lp through, (yo and through 2 lps on hook) 3 times.
2. Bptr (back post treble): Complete as for fptr, except insert hook from back to front to back.

Block (make 23):
Rnd 1: With gold, ch 8, join with sl st to form ring, ch 3, 2 dc in ring, (ch 3, 3 dc in ring) 3 times, ch 3, join with sl st in top of ch 3, fasten off.
Rnd 2: Join green in any ch-3 sp, ch 3, (2 dc, ch 3, 3 dc) in same sp, * fptr in next 3 dc, (3 dc, ch 3, 3 dc) in next corner sp, repeat from * 2 times, fptr in next 3 dc, join with sl st in top of beginning ch-3, fasten off.
Rnd 3: Join red in corner sp, ch 3, (2 dc, ch 3, 3 dc) in same sp, * bptr in next 3 dc, fptr in next 3 fptr, bptr in next 3 dc **, (3 dc, ch 3, 3 dc) in corner sp, repeat from *

2 times, repeat from * to ** once, join with sl st in beginning ch-3, fasten off.
Rnd 4: Join blue in any corner sp, ch 3, (2 dc, ch 3, 3 dc) in same sp, * (fptr in next 3 dc, bptr in next 3 bptr) 2 times, fptr in next 3 dc **, (3 dc, ch 3, 3 dc) in corner ch-3 sp, repeat from * 2 times, repeat from * to ** once, join with sl st in top of beginning ch-3, fasten off.
Sew 3 squares together in a row for center.

Lacy Insertion #1:
Rnd 1: Join blue in corner, working down long edge, ch 3, (2 dc, ch 3, 3 dc) in same sp, * [ch 3, sk next 3 sts, dc in next 3 sts] 3 times, ch 3, sk next 3 sts, dc in space before seam, dc in seam, dc in space after seam, repeat from * to last block, repeat from [to] 3 times, ch 3, sk next 3 sts, (3 dc, ch 3, 3 dc) in corner, repeat from [to] 3 times, ch 3, sk next 3 sts **, (3 dc, ch 3, 3 dc) in corner, repeat from 1st * to **, join with sl st in top of beginning ch-3.

Continued on page 131

Snuggle up with the colors of a rainbow! Strands of vivid colors are actually woven into a basic crocheted mesh to create this fabulous plaid blanket.

Woven Rainbow

By
ELEANOR ALBANO

Skill Level
Easy

Size
58" x 63"

Materials
4-ply worsted-weight yarn: 12 oz. yellow,
8 oz. each orange, red, rose, plum, purple,
royal blue, jade and hunter green
Hook size G/6 (4.50mm)

Gauge
5 sc rows = 1"; 4 sc sts = 1"

Instructions

Base Mesh:
Row 1: With yellow, ch 272, sc in 2nd ch from hook and in each sc across, turn.
Note: Ch 3 counts as 1st dc of each row.
Row 2: Ch 3, sk 1 st, dc in next st, (ch 1, sk 1 st, dc in next st) across, ending with dc in last st, turn.
Row 3: Ch 3, dc in next dc, (ch 1, dc in next dc) across, ending with dc in top of ch-3, turn.
Row 4: Repeat row 3, fasten off.
Rows 5-7: Join orange, repeat row 3, fasten off.
Rows 6-28: Repeat rows 5-7 in the following color order: red, rose, plum, purple, blue, jade, hunter green.
Continue in same manner, repeating colors until all colors have been used 6 times. Do not fasten off hunter green at end of last row, turn.
Final mesh row: Ch 1, sc in each dc and in each ch-1 sp across, fasten off, turn.

Weaving:
Test length needed for weaving by cutting 3 strands of yellow approximately 96" long. Thread 3 strands in yarn needle; start at right-hand side of afghan where hunter green ended. Insert needle from top into 1st mesh, under bar and up through 2nd mesh. Weave in this manner to opposite end of afghan. If at least 5" remains on each end of afghan after weaving, length is correct. Correct measurement as needed; cut 45 strands of each color.
To weave next row, insert needle from bottom into 1st mesh, over bar and down through 2nd mesh.
Alternate these 2 weaving rows using 3 strands each row, working 3 rows each color before changing colors. Repeat color order of base mesh until all colors have been used 5 times.
After weaving, lay afghan out flat on floor

Continued on page 131

Coral, aqua and a matching ombre yarn make a beautiful combination for bobble-studded triangles. It's an accent as fresh as a sea breeze in a bedroom or sun porch.

Bobbles & Triangles

By
ELEANOR ALBANO

Skill Level
Easy

Size
58" x 65½"

Materials
4-ply worsted-weight yarn: 30 oz. coral, blue and white ombre or variegated, 21 oz. white, 18 oz. each coral and blue
Hook size J/10 (6.00mm)

Gauge
6 sc = 2"; 4 sc rows = 1"

Instructions

Note: *Bobble: Retaining last lp of each dc on hook, 3 dc in indicated st, yo, draw through all lps on hook, ch 1.*

Triangle (make 70 ombre, 30 coral and 30 blue):
Row 1: Ch 22, sc in 2nd ch from hook and in each ch across, turn. (21)
Row 2: Ch 1, sc in each st across, turn.
Row 3: Ch 1, dec 1 sc over next 2 sc, sc in each sc across to within last 2 sc, dec 1 sc over last 2 sc, turn.
Row 4: Repeat row 2.
Row 5: Repeat row 3.
Row 6: Repeat row 2.
Row 7: Ch 1, dec 1 sc over 1st 2 sc, sc in next 3 sc, (bobble in next st, sc in next st) 4 times, sc in next 2 sc, dec 1 sc over last 2 sc, turn.
Row 8: Repeat row 2.
Row 9: Ch 1, dec 1 sc over 1st 2 sc, sc in next 3 sc, (bobble in next st, sc in next st) 3 times, sc in next 2 sc, dec 1 sc over last 2 sc, turn.

Row 10: Repeat row 2.
Row 11: Ch 1, dec 1 sc over 1st 2 sc, sc in next 3 sc, (bobble in next st, sc in next st) 2 times, sc in next 2 sc, dec 1 sc over last 2 sc, turn.
Row 12: Repeat row 2.
Row 13: Ch 1, dec 1 sc over 1st 2 sc, sc in next 3 sc, bobble in next st, sc in next 3 sc, dec 1 sc over last 2 sc, turn.
Rows 14-19: Repeat rows 2-3. (3)
Row 20: Ch 1, draw up a lp in each of next 3 sc, yo, draw through all lps on hook, fasten off.

Half-Triangles (make 10 coral and 10 blue):
Row 1: Ch 12, sc in 2nd ch from hook and in each ch across, turn.
Row 2: Ch 1, sc in each sc across, turn. (11)
Row 3: Ch 1, sc in each sc across to within last 2 sc, dec 1 sc over last 2 sc, turn.

Continued on page 130

Bobbles & Triangles

Continued from page 128

Rows 4-18: Repeat rows 2-3. (3)
Row 19: Ch 1, sc in next sc, dec 1 sc over last 2 sc, turn.
Row 20: Ch 1, sc in each of 2 sc, turn.
Row 21: Dec 1 sc over next 2 sc, fasten off.

Trim for Triangles and Half-Triangles:
Rnd 1: Join white in outer edge of triangle, ch 1, sc evenly spaced around, with sc in each of the 3 corners, join with sl st, fasten off.

Assembly:
Holding pieces right sides together, following diagram for placement of triangles and half-triangles, with white, working in back lps only, sew pieces together in strips, then sew strips together.

Border:
Rnd 1: Join white in outer edge of afghan, ch 1, sc in same st, sc evenly around, with 3 dc at corners and dc in each seam, join, fasten off.❈

BOBBLES & TRIANGLES

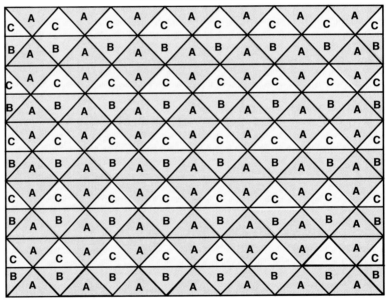

Crayon Blocks

Continued from page 124

Rnds 2-8: Sl st to corner ch-3 sp, ch 3, (2 dc, ch 3, 3 dc) in same sp, * ch 3, sk next 3 dc, 3 dc in next ch-3 sp, repeat from * to next corner sp, ch 3 **, (3 dc, ch 3, 3 dc) in corner sp, repeat from 1st * 2 times, repeat from 1st * to ** once, join with sl st in top of beginning ch-3. At end of row 8, fasten off.

Sew 3 blocks together in a row; sew to narrow end of center piece. Repeat for other end. Sew 7 blocks together in a row; sew to side, making sure end blocks of row are even with blocks on ends of center piece. Repeat for remaining side.

Lacy Insertion #2:

Rnds 1-8: Repeat rnds 1-8 of lacy insertion #1.

Border:

Rnd 1: Join gold in any corner sp, ch 3, (2 dc, ch 3, 3 dc) in same sp, * fptr in next 3 dc, 3 dc in next ch-3 sp, repeat from * to last 3 dc before corner sp, fptr in last 3 dc **, (3 dc, ch 3, 3 dc) in corner sp, repeat from 1st * 2 times, repeat from 1st * to ** once, join with sl st in top of ch-3, fasten off.

Rnd 2: Join green in any corner sp, ch 3, (2 dc, ch 3, 3 dc) in same corner sp, * bptr in next 3 sts, fptr in next 3 sts, repeat from * across to last 3 dc before corner sp, bptr in last 3 sts **, (3 dc, ch 3, 3 dc) in corner sp, repeat from 1st * 2 times, repeat from 1st * to ** once, join, fasten off.

Rnd 3: Join red in any corner sp, ch 3, (2 dc, ch 3, 3 dc) in same corner, * fptr in next 3 sts, bptr in next 3 sts, repeat from * across to last 3 dc before corner sp, fptr in last 3 sts **, (3 dc, ch 3, 3 dc) in corner sp, repeat from 1st * 2 times, repeat from 1st * once, join, fasten off.❀

Woven Rainbow

Continued from page 126

or bed to smooth all weaving.

Fringe:

Starting at left-hand side of afghan, knot 2 groups of 3 strands together. Repeat across until there are 3 groups left; knot these all together.

Now working from right to left, take 3 strands of first group and knot together with 3 strands of next group. Repeat across, leaving last 3 strands unknotted. Repeat for other end of afghan, trim fringe evenly to desired length.❀

Traditional Classics

Richly textured Aran designs are spectacular in crochet, as are favorite quilt block patterns. Time-honored classics find a place in every decor, and these afghans are perfect for warming up the nooks and crannies. Show off your crochet skills and decorating talents at the same time with a luxurious, off-white Irish fisherman afghan, a delicate filet tree design, or a wonderfully colorful quilt pattern.

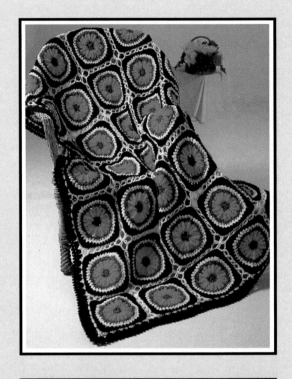

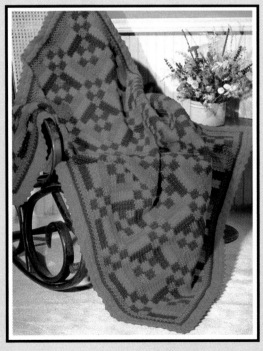

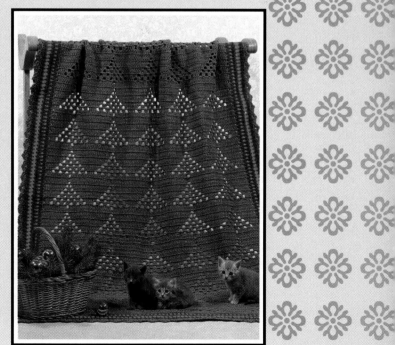

Curl up under a blanket of wildflowers! Motifs are crocheted together with a delicate white lace that beautifully highlights the vibrant hot-pink blossoms.

Wildflowers & Lace

By
ROSALIE DEVRIES

Skill Level
Challenging

Size
45" x 66"

Materials
4-ply worsted-weight yarn: 24 oz. hot pink, 20 oz.
reddish brown, 14 oz. white, 8 oz. green
Hook size F/5 (4.00mm)

Gauge
Block = 8" x 8"

Instructions

Rnd 1: With green, ch 4, 3 dc in 4th ch from hook, (drop lp from hook, insert hook in top of 1st ch, pulled dropped lp through, pull to tighten for popcorn st), * ch 3, 4 dc in same 1st ch, repeat from (to), repeat from * 4 times, ch 3, join with sl st in top of 1st pc, fasten off. (5 pc)

Rnd 2: Join pink in any ch-3 sp, ch 5, 3 dc in 4th ch from hook, repeat from (to) of rnd 1, [ch 4, 3 dc in top of pc, repeat from (to) of rnd 1] 5 times, sc in same ch-3 lp, ** repeat from [to] 5 times, sc in next ch-3 lp, repeat from [to] 5 times, sc in same ch-3 lp, repeat from ** 2 times, repeat from [to] 5 times, join with sl st in 1st ch of 1st ch-5, fasten off. (10 pc petals)

Rnd 3: Join green in center pc ch-4 of petal, ch 6, sc in same sp, * ch 5, sc in same sp, repeat from * once, *** ch 5, dc in 5th ch from hook, sc in center pc ch-4 of next petal, ** ch 5, sc in same sp, repeat from ** 2 times, repeat from *** 7 times, ch 5, dc in 5th ch from hook, join with sl st in 1st ch of 1st ch-6, fasten off. (40 lps)

Rnd 4: Join white in any lp, ch 3, dc in same lp, 2 dc in next lp and in each lp around, join with sl st in 3rd ch of ch-3, fasten off. (80)

Rnd 5: Join reddish brown in any dc, ch 4, * sk next 4 dc, sc in next dc, ch 3, repeat from * around, join with sl st in 1st ch of ch-4, do not fasten off.

Rnd 6: Sl st to next lp, ch 4, 6 tr in same lp, * 2 tr in next lp, 2 dc in next lp, 2 hdc in next lp, 2 sc in each of next 3 lps, 2 hdc in next lp, 2 dc in next lp, 2 tr in next lp, 7 tr in next lp, repeat from * around, join with sl st in 4th ch of beginning ch-4, fasten off.

Rnd 7 (first block only): Join white in center tr of any 7-tr group, ch 1, sc in same st, ch 9, sc in same st, *** sc in next 3 sts, * ch 3, sc in next 4 sts, repeat from * once, ch 3, sc in next 2 sts, ** ch 3, sc in next 4 sts, repeat from ** 2 times, ch 9, sc in same st, repeat from *** around, join with sl st in 1st sc, fasten off.

Continued on page 149

Rail Fence and Nine-Patch, two time-honored quilt designs, are combined in this terrific, show-stopping design. A scalloped edging contrasts beautifully with the geometric blocks.

Rail Fence Nine-Patch

By
KATHERINE ENG

Skill Level
Challenging

Size
46" x 58"

Materials
4-ply worsted-weight yarn: 21 oz. country red,
10½ oz. each pink and purple, 8 oz. burgundy, 7 oz. brown
Hook size F/5 (4.00mm)

Gauge
Each block = 3½" x 4"

Instructions

Notes:
1. Work each block individually, sl stitching together as you add one to the other.
2. Add blocks in rows beginning at bottom and working across from left to right.
3. Add 2nd and further rows of blocks across from left to right on top of the first row of blocks.
4. At end of each bar of rail fence blocks and each small square pattern for nine-patch blocks, after last sl st, pull yarn end through to the back and fasten off.

Block 1 (Vertical Rail Fence):
Vertical Bar #1:
Row 1: With brown, ch 6, sc in 2nd ch from hook, * ch 1, sk 1 ch, sc in next ch, repeat from * once, turn.
Row 2: Ch 1, sc in 1st sc, (ch 1, sk ch-1 sp, sc in next sc) across, turn.
Rows 3-15: Repeat row 2. At end of row 15, fasten off.
Vertical Bar #2:
Join country red in 5th ch at bottom of bar #1, ch 6.

Row 1: Repeat pattern of row 1 of bar #1; at end of row, sl st to row 1 of bar #1, sl st up 1 row on bar #1, turn.
Row 2: Repeat row 2 of bar #1.
Row 3: Repeat row 2 of bar #1; sl st to 3rd row of bar #1, sl st up 1 row on bar #1, turn.
Repeat rows 2-3 until 15 rows are completed. At end of row 15, fasten off.
Vertical Bar #3:
With burgundy, repeat bar #2.

Block 2 (Nine-Patch):
Square 1:
Join pink to 5th ch at bottom of bar #3, ch 6.
Rows 1-5: Repeat rows 1-5 of bar #2. At end of row 5, fasten off.
Square 2:
With purple, repeat square 1.
Square 3:
Work another small square across top of square 1, sl stitching to rows 6-10 of bar

Continued on page 140

Overlapping diamonds seem embossed on the smooth, afghan-stitch panels in a stunning design. Country blue, sage green and bone panels are trimmed with pastel peach.

Traditional Textures

By
INGEBORG M. KRAHN

Skill Level
Challenging

Size
54" x 64"

Materials
4-ply worsted-weight yarn: 21 oz. each off-white, country blue and sage green, 14 oz. peach, 10½ oz. bone
Afghan hook size I/9, crochet hook size H/8 (5.00mm) and tapestry needle

Gauge
16 sts and 13 rows afghan st = 4"

Instructions

Notes:
1. BAS (Basic Afghan Stitch): Each row is worked in two parts, pulling up lps and working them off the hook.
Row 1: *Using afghan hook, ch desired length. Keeping all lps on hook, pull up a lp in 2nd ch from hook and in each ch across; yo and draw through 1 lp, (yo and draw through 2 lps) until only 1 lp remains on hook. Last lp on hook is 1st lp of next row. Do not turn work.*
Row 2: *Keeping all lps on hook, draw up a lp in 2nd vertical bar and in each vertical bar across, yo and draw through 1 lp, (yo and draw through 2 lps) until 1 lp remains.*
Repeat row 2 for BAS.
2. FO (finish off): With beginning lp on hook, * insert hook from right to left in next vertical bar, yo, draw lp through bar and lp on hook, repeat from * across.
3. PC (popcorn): (Yo, insert hook into st, draw lp through, yo and draw through 1st 2 lps on hook) 2 times, yo and draw through next 2 lps on hook, push pc to right side.
4. PU (pick up): Pick up loop.

Panel (make 2 each off-white, blue and green; make 1 bone):
Row 1: With afghan hook, ch 23, work in BAS. (23)
Rows 2-4: Work in BAS.
Row 5: Following graph, PU 1st 11 sts in BAS, PC in next st, PU last 11 sts in BAS.
Row 6: Following graph, PU 1st 10 sts in BAS, PC in next st, PU next st in BAS, PC in next st, PU last 10 sts in BAS.
Rows 7-45: Follow graph to complete 1 pattern repeat.
Rows 46-197: Repeat rows 6-45 3 times and rows 6-37 once.
Rows 198-201: Work in BAS.
Row 202: FO, ch 1, fasten off.

Continued on page 141

Rail Fence Nine-Patch

Continued from page 137

#3; fasten off.

Squares 4-6:
Join red to 5th ch at bottom of square 2, ch 6. Repeat squares 2-3 for squares 4-5. For square 6, ch 1, work across top of square 3 attaching with sl st to rows 11-15 of bar #3; fasten off.

Squares 7-8:
Join purple in end sc of square 4, ch 1, work pattern across top of square 4 attaching with sl st to side of square 5, ch 1, work across top of square 5 attaching with sl st to side of square 6; fasten off.

Square 9:
Join pink in end sc of square 7, ch 1, work pattern across, sl st to side of square 8; fasten off.

Block 3 (Vertical Rail Fence):
Add 3 vertical bars in the same manner as bar #2 to the right of nine-patch, sl stitching rows of 1st bar to side of nine-patch. Make 1st bar with brown, 2nd bar with red and 3rd bar with burgundy as before.

Remaining Blocks:
Continue adding nine-patch and vertical rail fence blocks to the right until there are 6 rail fence and 5 nine-patch blocks across (11 blocks).

Row 2 of Blocks:
Block 12 (Nine-Patch):
Work nine-patch over top of vertical bars of beginning block, working square 1 on top of brown bar, square 2 on top of red bar, and so on.

Block 13 (Horizontal Rail Fence):
Horizontal Bar #1:
Join brown in end sc of nine-patch (over pink).
Row 1: Ch 1, sc in 1st sc, (ch 1, sk ch-1 sp, sc in next sc) 2 times, ch 1, sk joining between bars, sc in next sc, repeat from * to * once, sl st to row 1 of nine-patch, sl st up 1 row, turn. (9 sc and 8 ch-1)
Row 2: Ch 1, repeat pattern across, turn.
Rows 3-5: Repeat pattern, sl stitching to corresponding rows of nine-patch; fasten off.

Horizontal Bars #2 and 3:
With red and burgundy, work as for bar #1.

Remaining Blocks:
Continue working nine-patch and horizontal rail fence blocks across for 2nd row of blocks.

Remaining Rows:
Begin row 3 with vertical rail fence block over tops of small squares of nine-patch. Begin 1st square of nine-patch on burgundy bar 3 sc from the left edge, 2nd square 3 sc to the right, and so on. Continue adding blocks until 14 rows are completed.

Border:
Rnd 1: Join pink in any st along edge, ch 1, sc evenly spaced around, with sc in each of 15 sts along each block edge and 3 sc in each corner of afghan, join with sl st, turn.
Rnd 2: Ch 1, sc in 1st sc, (ch 1, sk 1 sc, sc in next sc) around, with 3 sc in each corner, adjusting if necessary by not skipping 1 st before corner to make pattern come out evenly, join with sl st, turn.
Rnd 3: Ch 1, sc in each sc and in each ch-1 sp around, with 3 sc in each corner, join, turn.
Rnd 4: Repeat rnd 2, fasten off, turn.
Rnd 5: Join purple in any ch-1 sp, ch 3, dc in same st, (2 dc in next ch-1 sp) around, with 5 dc in each corner, join with sl st in top of ch-3, fasten off, do not turn.
Rnd 6: Join red, ch 1, sc in each dc around, with 3 sc in each corner, join, turn.
Rnd 7: Ch 1, sc in 1st sc, (sk 1 sc, 3 dc in next sc, sk 1 sc, sc in next sc) around, with sc in 1st sc at corner, 3 dc in center sc at corner, sc in last st at corner, adjusting if necessary as in rnd 2, join, turn.
Rnd 8: Ch 3, 2 dc in same sc, (sc in center dc of 3-dc group, 3 dc in next sc) around, join, sl st into sc, turn.
Rnd 9: Ch 3, repeat rnd 8, working 5 dc in each center corner st, join, turn.
Rnd 10 (right side): Sl st in sc and 1st dc,

ch 1, * sc in 1st dc of 3-dc group, (sc, ch 3, sc) in center dc, sc in 3rd dc of group, sk next sc, repeat from * around, with [sc in sc before corner 5-dc group, (sc, ch 3, sc)

in 1st dc, sc in 2nd dc, (sc, ch 3, sc) in center dc, sc in 4th dc, (sc, ch 3, sc) in 5th dc, sc in next sc] in corners, join with sl st, fasten off.❈

Traditional Textures

Continued from page 138

Panel Trim:

Rnd 1: With right side of panel facing up, turn panel sideways, with H hook, join peach in back lp of 1st st (not foundation ch) of row 1, ch 1, sc in same st, sc in back lp of next 3 sts (rows), * (dc in next vertical bar of 2nd st from edge) 2 times, sk sts behind dcs, sc in back lp of next 3 sts, repeat from * to last st, sc in back lp of last st, (sc, ch 2, sc) in 1st FO st (corner), sc in next 3 sts, tr in 2nd vertical bar down of next 2 sts, sk sts behind trs, sc in next 4 sts, tr in 2nd vertical bar down of next 3 sts, sk sts behind trs, sc in next 4 sts, tr in 2nd vertical bar down of next 2 sts, sk sts behind trs, sc in next 3 sts, (sc, ch 2, sc) in ch-1 of last FO st, sc in back lps of next 4 sts down side, repeat from 1st * down side and across bottom, with corners worked in 1st and last ch and sc worked in foundation ch, join with sl st in 1st sc, fasten off, do not turn.

Rnd 2: Join color matching panel in joining, ch 1, sc in same st, * dc in front lps of next 3 sts, sc in next 2 dc, repeat from * to last 5 sts, dc in next 3 front lps, sk sts behind dcs, sc in next 2 sts, (sc, ch 2, sc) in corner ch-2 sp, sc in next sc, tr in 1st vertical bar down on next 3 sts, sc in next 2 tr, tr in 1st vertical bar down of next 4 sts, sc in next 3 tr, tr in first vertical bar down of next 4 sts, sc in next 2 tr, tr in 1st vertical bar down of next 3 sts, sk scs behind trs, sc in next sc, (sc, ch 2, sc) in corner ch-2 sp, sc in next 2 sc down side, repeat from 1st * around, join, do not turn.

Rnd 3: Ch 1, sc in same st, sc in each st around, with (sc, ch 2, sc) in corners, join, fasten off.

Rnd 4: Join peach in any sc, ch 1, repeat rnd 3, fasten off.

Assembly:

Join panels in the following order: green,

off-white, blue, bone, green, off-white, blue. Holding wrong sides together and working through back lps only of both thicknesses, join peach in ch-2 sp in corner, ch 2, matching sts of panels, * insert hook in back lps of next sts, yo, draw lp through, ch 1, repeat from * across, fasten off.

Edging:

Rnd 1: Join peach in any st along edge, sc in each st around, with (sc, ch 2, sc) in each corner sp, join.

Rnd 2: Continuing with peach, repeat rnd 1.❈

STITCH KEY	
☐	st
◉	pc

TRADITIONAL TEXTURES

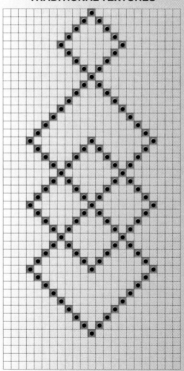

Perky tassels add the finishing touch to this quilt-like afghan. The traditional navy and white color scheme blends beautifully with warm wood tones and country decor.

Quilted Stars

By
CHRISTINA MCNEESE

Skill Level
Average

Size
52" x 86"

Materials
4-ply worsted-weight yarn: 48 oz. white, 28 oz. navy
Hook size G/6 (4.50mm)

Gauge
7 sc = 2½"; 6 sc rows = 2"

Instructions

Note: *Crochet over yarn strand not in use at all times. Turn each row.*

Row 1: With white, ch 145, sc in 2nd ch from hook and in next 11 sc, (with navy, sc in 12 sts, with white, sc in next 24 sts) across, ending with 12 white sc.

Row 2: Ch 1, (13 white sc, 10 navy sc, 13 white sc) 4 times.

Row 3: Ch 1, (14 white sc, 8 navy sc, 14 white sc) 4 times.

Row 4: Ch 1, (15 white sc, 6 navy sc, 15 white sc) 4 times.

Row 5: Ch 1, (16 white sc, 4 navy sc, 16 white sc) 4 times.

Row 6: Ch 1, (17 white sc, 2 navy sc, 17 white sc) 4 times.

Row 7: Ch 1, (12 white sc, 1 navy sc, 10 white sc, 1 navy sc, 12 white sc) 4 times.

Row 8: Ch 1, (12 white sc, 2 navy sc, 8 white sc, 2 navy sc, 12 white sc) 4 times.

Row 9: Ch 1, (12 white sc, 3 navy sc, 6 white sc, 3 navy sc, 12 white sc) 4 times.

Row 10: Ch 1, (12 white sc, 4 navy sc, 4 white sc, 4 navy sc, 12 white sc) 4 times.

Row 11: Ch 1, (12 white sc, 5 navy sc, 2 white sc, 5 navy sc, 12 white sc) 4 times.

Row 12: Ch 1, (12 white sc, 12 navy sc, 12 white sc) 4 times.

Row 13: Ch 1, (1 navy sc, 5 white sc, 24 navy sc, 5 white sc, 1 navy sc) 4 times.

Row 14: Ch 1, (2 navy sc, 5 white sc, 22 navy sc, 5 white sc, 2 navy sc) 4 times.

Row 15: Ch 1, (3 navy sc, 5 white sc, 20 navy sc, 5 white sc, 3 navy sc) 4 times.

Row 16: Ch 1, (4 navy sc, 5 white sc, 18 navy sc, 5 white sc, 4 navy sc) 4 times.

Row 17: Ch 1, (5 navy sc, 5 white sc, 16 navy sc, 5 white sc, 5 navy sc) 4 times.

Row 18: Ch 1, (6 navy sc, 5 white sc, 14 navy sc, 5 white sc, 6 navy sc) 4 times.

Rows 19-35: Working backward numerically, repeat rows 18-2.

Rows 36-37: Ch 1, (12 white sc, 12 navy sc, 12 white sc) 4 times.

Rows 38-180: Repeat rows 2-37.
At end of row 180, fasten off.

Continued on page 153

This bold and beautiful blanket is made with simple single crochet in three strips of three blocks each. The result is a smoothly textured afghan that drapes beautifully.

Contemporary Blocks

By
COATS & CLARK

Skill Level
Easy

Size
52" x 54"

Materials
4-ply worsted-weight yarn: 16 oz. each pink, mint and black
Hook size G/6 (4.50mm)

Gauge
4 sc = 1"; 4 rows = 1"

Instructions

Strip A (make 2):
Pattern #1:
Row 1: With mint, ch 21, with pink, ch 21, with mint, ch 22, sc in 2nd ch from hook, sc in 20 ch with mint, sc in 21 ch with pink, sc in 21 ch with mint, turn. (63)
Row 2: Ch 1, 21 mint sc, 21 pink sc, 21 mint sc, turn.
Rows 3-24: Repeat row 2.
Row 25: Ch 1, 21 pink sc, 21 black sc, 21 pink sc, turn.
Rows 26-48: Repeat row 25.
Rows 49-72: Repeat row 2.
Pattern #2:
Row 73: Join black, ch 1, sc in each sc across, turn.
Rows 74-80: Repeat row 73.
Rows 81-96: Ch 1, 8 black sc, 47 mint sc, 8 black sc, turn.
Rows 97-120: Ch 1, 8 black sc, 12 mint sc, 23 black sc, 12 mint sc, 8 black sc, turn.
Rows 121-136: Repeat rows 81-96.
Rows 137-144: Repeat rows 73-80.
Pattern #1:
Row 145: Join mint, ch 1, 21 mint sc, 21 pink sc, 21 mint sc, turn.

Rows 146-216: Repeat rows 2-72. At end of row 216, fasten off.

Strip B (make 1):
Pattern #3:
Row 1: With black ch 64, sc in 2nd ch from hook and in each ch across, turn. (63)
Rows 2-72: Substituting pink for mint, repeat rows 74-144.
Pattern #1:
Rows 73-144: Repeat rows 145-216 of strip A, pattern #1.
Pattern #3:
Row 145: Repeat row 73 of strip A.
Rows 146-216: Repeat rows 2-72 above. At end of row 216, fasten off.

Assembly:
Aligning rows exactly, sew one A strip to each side of B strip.

Border:
Rnd 1: Join black at side edge, ch 2, hdc evenly spaced around entire outer edge, with (hdc, ch 2, hdc) in each corner, join, fasten off.❊

Traditional Aran cables, popcorns and other patterned stitches are shown to their best advantage in classic off-white in this luxurious heirloom afghan.

Irish Fisherman

By
BONNIE FRIDLEY

Skill Level
Challenging

Size
53" x 63" plus fringe

Materials
4-ply worsted-weight yarn: 80 oz. fisherman
Hook size J/10 (6.00mm)

Gauge
5 sc = 1½"; 5 sc rows = 1½"

Instructions

Notes:
1. When working fpdc in row below, draw yarn up even with work.
2. Pc (popcorn): Work 3 sc in indicated st, remove hook, insert hook in 1st sc, pick up dropped lp, draw through, ch 1.

Panel A (make 2):
Row 1: Ch 41, sc in 2nd ch from hook and in each ch across, turn. (40)
Row 2 and all even-numbered rows: Ch 1, sc in each sc across, turn.
Row 3: Ch 1, sc in next sc, fpdc around next sc of row 1, sk sc behind fpdc, * sc in next 3 sc, fpdc around next sc of row 1, sk sc behind fpdc, repeat from * across, ending with sc in last 2 sts, turn.
Row 5: Ch 1, sc in next 2 sc, fpdc around fpdc below, sk sc behind fpdc, sc in next sc, fpdc around next fpdc below, sk sc behind fpdc, * sc in next sc, fpdc around same fpdc as last fpdc, sk sc behind fpdc, sc in next sc, fpdc around next fpdc, sk sc behind fpdc, repeat from * across, ending with sc in last 3 sc, turn.

Row 7: Ch 1, * sc in next 3 sc, (yo, insert hook around next fpdc and draw up a lp) 2 times (5 lps on hook), yo, draw through 4 lps, yo, draw through remaining 2 lps (double fpdc made), sk 1 sc behind double fpdc, repeat from * across, ending with sc in next 4 sc, turn.
Row 9: Ch 1, sc in next 2 sc, * fpdc around fpdc below, sk sc behind fpdc, sc in next sc, fpdc around same fpdc as last fpdc, sk sc behind fpdc, repeat from * across, ending with sc in last 3 sc, turn.
Row 11: Ch 1, sc in next sc, fpdc around fpdc below, sk sc behind fpdc, * sc in each of next 3 sc, fpdc around fpdc below, sk sc behind fpdc, repeat from * across, ending with sc in next 2 sc, turn.
Repeat rows 4-11 until 220 rows are completed.
Row 221: Repeat row 9.
Row 222: Ch 1, sc in each sc across, turn.

Panel B (make 2):
Row 1: Ch 36, sc in 2nd ch from hook and
Continued on next page

Irish Fisherman

Continued from page 147

in each ch across, turn. (35)

Row 2: Ch 1, sc in next 7 sts, (pc in next st, sc in next 9 sts) 2 times, pc in next st, sc in next 7 sts, turn.

Row 3 and all odd-numbered rows: Ch 1, sc in each sc across, turn.

Row 4: Ch 1, sc in next 6 sts, (pc in next st, sc in next st, pc in next st, sc in next 7 sts) 2 times, pc in next st, sc in next st, pc in next st, sc in next 6 sts, turn.

Row 6: Ch 1, sc in next 5 sts, (pc in next st, sc in next 3 sts, pc in next st, sc in next 5 sts) 2 times, pc in next st, sc in next 3 sts, pc in next st, sc in next 5 sts, turn.

Row 8: Ch 1, sc in next 4 sts, (pc in next st, sc in next 5 sts, pc in next st, sc in next 3 sts) 2 times, pc in next st, sc in next 5 sts, pc in next st, sc in next 4 sts, turn.

Row 10: Ch 1, sc in next 3 sts, (pc in next st, sc in next 7 sts, pc in next st, sc in next st) 2 times, pc in next st, sc in next 7 sts, pc in next st, sc in next 3 sts, turn.

Row 12: Ch 1, sc in next 2 sts, (pc in next st, sc in next 9 sts) 2 times, pc in next st, sc in next 2 sts, turn.

Row 14: Repeat row 10.

Row 16: Repeat row 8.

Row 18: Repeat row 6.

Row 20: Repeat row 4.

Row 22: Repeat row 2.

Repeat rows 4-22 until 221 rows are completed.

Row 222: Ch 1, sc in each sc across, turn.

Panel C (make 1):

Row 1: Ch 36, sc in 2nd ch from hook and in each ch across, turn. (35)

Row 2: Ch 1, sc in next 7 sts, (pc in next st, sc in next 9 sts) 2 times, sc in next 7 sts, turn.

Row 3 and all odd-numbered rows: Ch 1, sc in each sc across, turn.

Row 4: Ch 1, sc in next 6 sts, (pc in next st, sc in next st, pc in next st, sc in next 7 sts) 2 times, pc in next st, sc in next st, pc in next st, sc in next 6 sts, turn.

Row 6: Ch 1, sc in next 5 sts, (pc in next st, sc in next 3 sts, pc in next st, sc in next 5 sts) 3 times, turn.

Row 8: Ch 1, sc in next 4 sts, (pc in next

st, sc in next 2 sts, fpdc around sc 2 rows below, sk sc behind fpdc, sc in next 2 sts, pc in next st, sc in next 3 sts) 3 times, sc in last sc, turn.

Row 10: Ch 1, sc in next 3 sts, (pc in next st, sc in next 2 sts, fpdc around fpdc below, sk sc behind fpdc, sc in next st, fpdc around same fpdc below, sk sc behind fpdc, sc in next 2 sts, pc in next st, sc in next st) 3 times, sc in last 2 scs, turn.

Row 12: Ch 1, sc in next 2 sts, (pc in next st, sc in next 2 sts, fpdc around fpdc, sk sc behind fpdc, sc in next 3 sts, fpdc around next fpdc, sk sc behind fpdc, sc in next 2 sts) 3 times, pc in next st, sc in last 2 scs, turn.

Row 14: Ch 1, sc in next 3 sts, (pc in next st, sc in next 2 sts, fpdc around fpdc, sk sc behind fpdc, sc in next st, fpdc around next fpdc, sk sc behind fpdc, sc in next 2 sts) 3 times, sc in next 2 scs, turn.

Row 16: Ch 1, sc in next 4 sts, * pc in next st, sc in next 2 sts, (yo, insert hook around next fpdc and draw up a lp) 2 times (5 lps on hook), yo, draw through 4 lps, yo, draw through remaining 2 lps (double fpdc made), sk 1 sc behind double fpdc, sc in next 2 sts, pc in next st, sc in next 3 sts, repeat from * once, pc in next st, sc in next 2 sts, (yo, insert hook around next fpdc and draw up a lp) 2 times (5 lps on hook), yo, draw through 4 lps, yo, draw through remaining 2 lps (double fpdc made), sk 1 sc behind double fpdc, sc in next 2 sts, pc in next st, sc in next 4 sts, turn.

Row 18: Ch 1, sc in next 5 sts, (pc in next st, sc in next st, fpdc around fpdc, sk sc behind fpdc, sc in next st, pc in next st, sc in next 2 sts, fpdc around sc 2 rows below, sk sc behind fpdc, sc in next 2 sts) 2 times, pc in next st, sc in next st, fpdc around fpdc, sk sc behind fpdc, sc in next st, pc in next st, sc in next 5 sts, turn.

Row 20: Ch 1, sc in next 6 sts, (pc in next st, sc in next st, fpdc around fpdc, sk sc behind fpdc, sc in next st, fpdc around same fpdc as last fpdc, sk sc behind fpdc, sc in next 2 sts) 2 times, pc in next st, sc in next st, pc in next st, sc in next 6 sts, turn.

Row 22: Ch 1, sc in next 7 sts, (pc in next st, sc in next 2 sts, fpdc around fpdc, sk sc behind fpdc, sc in next 3 sts, fpdc around fpdc, sk sc behind fpdc, sc in next 2 sts) 2 times, pc in next st, sc in next 7 sts, turn.

Row 24: Ch 1, sc in next 6 sts, (pc in next st, sc in next st, pc in next st, sc in next 2 sts, fpdc around fpdc, sk sc behind fpdc, sc in next st, fpdc around fpdc, sk sc behind fpdc, sc in next 2 sts) 2 times, pc in next st, sc in next st, pc in next st, sc in next 6 sts, turn.

Row 26: Ch 1, sc in next 5 sts, * pc in next st, sc in next 3 sts, pc in next st, sc in next 2 sts, (yo, insert hook around next fpdc and draw up a lp) 2 times (5 lps on hook), yo, draw through 4 lps, yo, draw through remaining 2 lps (double fpdc made), sk 1 sc behind double fpdc, sc in next 2 sts, repeat from * once, pc in next st, sc in next 3 sts, pc in next st, sc in next 5 sts, turn.

Row 28: Ch 1, sc in next 4 sts, (pc in next st, sc in next 2 sts, fpdc around sc 2 rows below, sk sc behind fpdc, sc in next 2 sts, pc in next st, sc in next st, fpdc around fpdc, sk sc behind fpdc, sc in next sc) 2 times, pc in next st, sc in next 2 sts, fpdc around sc 2 rows below, sk sc behind fpdc, sc in next 2 sts, pc in next st, sc in next 4 sts, turn.

Repeat rows 9-28 until 221 rows are completed.

Row 222: Ch 1, sc in each sc across, fasten off.

Assembly:
Holding wrong sides of panels A and B together, join yarn to right side of work and working through both thicknesses, sc evenly spaced across edge, fasten off. Holding wrong side of panel C to B, join in same manner.

Join panels in same manner for completed afghan with panels in the following order: A, B, C, B, A.

Fringe:
For each fringe, cut five 15" strands of yarn. Insert hook in 1st st at end of afghan, draw 1 cut end of 5 strands through. Insert hook in next st, draw remaining cut ends of same fringe through; pull ends even. Insert hook at center of fringe and draw up a lp, draw all 10 cut ends through lp, pull to secure. (Sk 2 sts, repeat fringe in next 2 sts) across; repeat for opposite end of afghan. Trim ends evenly.❁

Wildflowers & Lace
Continued from page 135

Make 39 more blocks with rnds 1-6; join together using following rnd 7:

Rnd 7 (joining rnd): Join white in center tr of 7-tr group on 2nd block, ch 1, sc in same sp, ch 4, sc in corner ch-9 lp of 1st block, ch 4, sc in same sp on 2nd block, sc in next 3 sc on 2nd block, * [ch 1, sc in next ch-3 lp of 2nd block, ch 1, sc in next 4 sts of 2nd block, repeat from * once, ch 1, sc in next ch-3 lp of 2nd block, ch 1, sc in next 2 sts of 2nd block, ** ch 1, sc in next ch-3 lp of 1st block, ch 1, sc in next 4 sts of 2nd block, repeat from ** 2 times, ch 4, sc in next corner lp of 1st block, ch 4, sc in same sp on 2nd block, sc in next 3 sts of 2nd block.

For blocks joined to other blocks on two sides, repeat from [once, complete rnd on 2nd block as previously instructed, fasten off.

Border:
Rnd 1: Join reddish brown in any corner ch-9 lp, 10 tr in same lp, [5 tr in each of next 2 lps, 3 tr in each of next 2 lps, 5 tr in next 2 lps to next corner, 11 tr in corner lp], repeat from [to] around, join with sl st in 4th ch of 1st ch-4.

Rnd 2: Ch 4, * sk next st, ch 3, repeat from * around, join with sl st in 1st ch of 1st ch-4.

Rnd 3: Sl st to next lp, ch 1, sc in same lp, * ch 3, sl st in 3rd lp from hook (picot made), sc in same lp, sc in next lp, repeat from * around, join with sl st in 1st sc, fasten off.❁

Juniper Trees

By
KATHERINE ENG

Skill Level
Easy

Size
41" x 55"

Materials
4-ply worsted-weight yarn: 23 oz. juniper,
5½ oz. dark juniper, 2 oz. bright red
Hook size F/5 (4.00mm)

Gauge
4 dc = 1"; 2 dc rows = 1"

Instructions

Notes:
1. Ch 3 at beginning of row counts as 1st dc.
2. Row 1 is right side of afghan.

Row 1: With juniper, ch 136, dc in 4th ch from hook and in each ch across, turn. (134)

Row 2: Ch 3, dc in next 13 dc, (ch 2, sk 2 dc, dc in next 24 dc) 4 times, ch 2, sk 2 dc, dc in next 14 dc, turn.

Row 3: Ch 3, dc in next 3 dc, * ch 2, sk 2 dc, (3 dc in next dc, ch 1, sk 3 dc) 2 times, 3 dc in next ch-2 sp, (ch 1, sk 3 dc, 3 dc in next dc) 2 times, ch 2, sk 2 dc, dc in next 4 dc, repeat from * 4 times, turn.

Row 4: Ch 3, dc in next 3 dc, * 2 dc in next ch-2 sp, ch 2, 3 dc in next ch-1 sp, (ch 1, 3 dc in next ch-1 sp) 3 times, ch 2, 2 dc in next ch-2 sp, dc in next 4 sts, repeat from * 4 times, turn.

Row 5: Ch 3, dc in next 5 dc, * 2 dc in next ch-2 sp, ch 2, 3 dc in next ch-1 sp, (ch 1, 3 dc in next ch-1 sp) 2 times, ch 2,

2 dc in next ch-2 sp, dc in next 8 dc, repeat from * 3 times, 2 dc in next ch-2 sp, ch 2, 3 dc in next ch-1 sp, (ch 1, 3 dc in next ch-1 sp) 2 times, ch 2, 2 dc in next ch-2 sp, dc in next 6 dc, turn.

Row 6: Ch 3, dc in next 7 dc, * 2 dc in next ch-2 sp, ch 2, 3 dc in next ch-1 sp, ch 1, 3 dc in next ch-1 sp, ch 2, 2 dc in next ch-2 sp, dc in next 12 dc, repeat from * 3 times, 2 dc in next ch-2 sp, ch 2, 3 dc in next ch-1 sp, ch 1, 3 dc in next ch-1 sp, ch 2, 2 dc in next ch-2 sp, dc in next 8 dc, turn.

Row 7: Dc in next 9 dc, * 2 dc in next ch-2 sp, ch 2, 3 dc in next ch-1 sp, ch 2, 2 dc in next ch-2 sp, dc in next 16 dc, repeat from * 3 times, 2 dc in next ch-2 sp, ch 2, 3 dc in next ch-1 sp, ch 2, 2 dc in next ch-2 sp, dc in next 10 dc, turn.

Row 8: Ch 3, dc in next 11 dc, * dc in next ch-2 sp, ch 2, dc in center dc of next 3-dc group, ch 2, dc in next ch-2 sp, dc in next 20 dc, repeat from * 3 times, dc in

Continued on page 152

Juniper Trees

Continued from page 150

next ch-2 sp, ch 2, dc in center dc of next 3-dc group, ch 2, dc in next ch-2 sp, dc in next 12 dc, turn.

Row 9: Ch 3, dc in next 12 dc, * dc in next ch-2 sp, ch 2, dc in next ch-2 sp, dc in next 22 dc, repeat from * 3 times, dc in next ch-2 sp, ch 2, dc in next ch-2 sp, dc in next 13 dc, turn.

Row 10: Ch 3, dc in each dc and 2 dc in each ch-2 sp across, turn. (134)
Repeat rows 2-10 10 times.
At end of last repeat, fasten off.

Border:

Rnd 1 (right side): Working across top of afghan, sc in each dc across, ending with (sc, ch 2, sc) in last dc for corner; working down side, (ch 1, sk edge of dc, sc in top of next dc) across, ending with (sc, ch 2, sc) in end ch; working across bottom, sc in each st across, with (sc, ch 2, sc) in corner; working down remaining side, (ch 1, sk edge of next dc, sc in top of same dc) across, ending with (sc, ch 2) in same dc as beginning st, join, fasten off, turn.

Rnd 2: Join dk. juniper in any ch-1 sp on edge, ch 1, sc in each ch-1 sp and in each sc around, with (sc, ch 2, sc) in each corner, join, turn.

Note: In order for pattern to come out evenly, work (ch 1, sc in next sc) as needed near corner.

Rnd 3: Ch 1, sc in next sc, (ch 1, sk next sc, sc in next sc) around, with [ch 1, sk 1 sc, (sc, ch 2, sc) in ch-2 sp] in corners, join, fasten off, turn.

Rnd 4: Join red in any ch-1 sp on side edge, ch 1, sc in same sp, (ch 1, sk next sc, sc in ch-1 sp) around, [ch 1, sk 1 sc, (sc, ch 2, sc) in ch-2 sp] in corners, join, fasten off, turn.

Rnd 5 (right side): Join dk. juniper in any ch-1 sp, ch 3, dc in same sp, 2 dc in each ch-1 sp around and (2 dc, ch 2, 2 dc) in corners, join with sl st in top of ch-3, turn.

Rnd 6: Ch 1, sc in space between groups of 2 dc, ch 1, sk 2 dc, (sc in sp between dcs, ch 1, sk 2 dc) around, with [ch 1, sk 2 dc, (sc, ch 2, sc) in ch-2 sp] in corners, join, fasten off, turn.

Rnd 7: With red, repeat rnd 5.

Rnd 8: With dk. juniper, repeat rnd 6.

Rnd 9: Ch 1, sc in ch-1 sp, ch 1, sk 1 sc, (sc in next ch-1 sp, ch 1, sk 1 sc) around, with (sc, ch 2, sc) in corners, join, turn.

Rnd 10: Ch 1, sc in each sc and in each ch-1 sp around, with (sc, ch 2, sc) in corners, join, fasten off.

Rnd 11 (right side): Join juniper in 8th sc to the left of any corner, ch 1, sc in same sc, [sk 2 sc, (2 dc, ch 2, 2 dc) in next sc (shell made), sk 2 sc, sc in next sc] around, with [sk 1 sc, (3 dc, ch 2, 3 dc) in ch-2 sp, sk 1 sc, sc in next sc] in each corner, join, do not turn.

Rnd 12 (right side): Ch 1, sc in same st, * ch 3, (sc, ch 3, sc) in next shell, ch 3, sc in next sc, repeat from * around, with [ch 3, sc in same sc, ch 3, (sc, ch 3, sc) in ch-2 sp in corner, ch 3, (sc, ch 3, sc) in next sc] in each corner, join, fasten off.✸

Quilted Stars

Continued from page 142

Fringe:

For each fringe, cut twelve 14" strands of yarn; fold strands in half, draw fold through st at bottom of afghan, draw cut ends through fold, pull to secure. Attach 9 fringes evenly spaced across top and bottom edges, alternating white and navy as shown in photo.❈

General Instructions

Yarn

Yarn for afghans is usually baby-weight, sport-weight, worsted-weight or bulky. By using the weight of yarn specified in the pattern, you will be assured of achieving proper gauge.

Hooks

Crochet hooks are sized for different weights of yarn, and are available in plastic, wood, aluminum and steel. Most afghans are made with medium and large hooks in plastic, aluminum or wood. Afghan hooks are similar to knitting needles, except they have a hook at one end.

The hook size suggested in the pattern is to be used as a guide for determining the size hook to use. The gauge is more important in a pattern than the specified hook size.

Gauge

The purpose for checking gauge is to determine which hook size to use. The tightness or looseness of your stitches determines gauge, and is affected by hook size. Gauge is measured by counting the number of stitches or rows per inch.

Parentheses, Asterisks and More

For clarity, written instructions may include symbols such as parentheses, asterisks, brackets and diamonds. These symbols are used as signposts to set off a portion of instructions which are to be worked more than once.

Joining and Sewing

For joining pieces with crochet, hold pieces wrong sides together and sl st or sc together.

To join with whipstitch, hold pieces wrong sides together and with a large yarn needle, beginning in one corner and matching stitches, sew pieces together.

Blocking

Most afghans do not require professional blocking. To smooth out puckers at seams and to give a more finished appearance, a light steam pressing works well. Lay afghan on carpeting, bed or large table. Shape and smooth with hands as much as possible. Set iron on medium or permanent press and hold iron slightly above stitches, allowing steam to penetrate stitches. Do not rest iron on stitches. Allow to cool and dry completely.

If you prefer professional blocking, choose a cleaning service that specializes in needlework. Request blocking only if you do not want the afghan dry-cleaned. For best results, attach fringe after professional blocking.

Standard Stitch Abbreviations	
ch(s)	chain(s)
dc	double crochet
dtr	double treble crochet
hdc	half double crochet
lp(s)	loop(s)
rnd(s)	round(s)
sc	single crochet
sl st	slip stitch
sp(s)	space(s)
st(s)	stitch(es)
tog	together
tr	treble
tr tr	triple treble
yo	yarn over

Stitch Guide

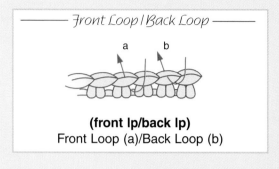

(front lp/back lp)
Front Loop (a)/Back Loop (b)

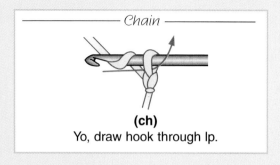

(ch)
Yo, draw hook through lp.

Slip Stitch

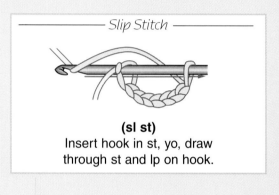

(sl st)
Insert hook in st, yo, draw
through st and lp on hook.

Single Crochet

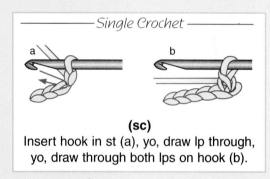

(sc)
Insert hook in st (a), yo, draw lp through,
yo, draw through both lps on hook (b).

Half Double Crochet

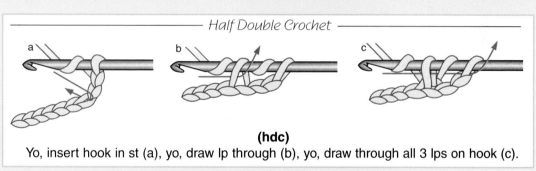

(hdc)
Yo, insert hook in st (a), yo, draw lp through (b), yo, draw through all 3 lps on hook (c).

Double Crochet

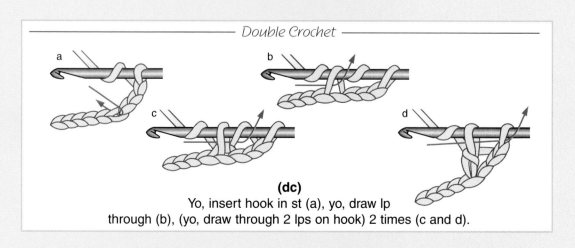

(dc)
Yo, insert hook in st (a), yo, draw lp
through (b), (yo, draw through 2 lps on hook) 2 times (c and d).

Treble Crochet

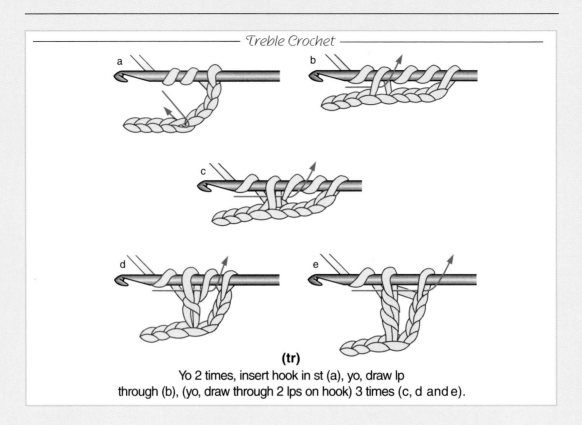

(tr)
Yo 2 times, insert hook in st (a), yo, draw lp
through (b), (yo, draw through 2 lps on hook) 3 times (c, d and e).

Double Treble Crochet

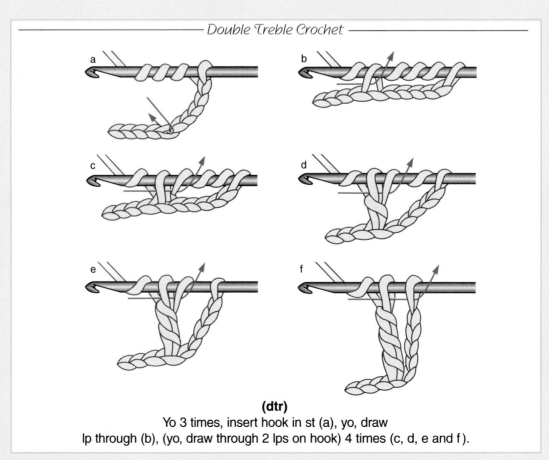

(dtr)
Yo 3 times, insert hook in st (a), yo, draw
lp through (b), (yo, draw through 2 lps on hook) 4 times (c, d, e and f).

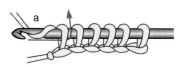 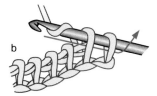

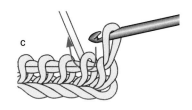 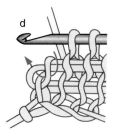

(afghan st)

Row 1: Chain number indicated in pattern, insert hook in 2nd ch from hook, yo, draw up ¼" lp, (insert hook in next ch, yo, draw up ¼" lp) across, leaving all lps on hook, **do not** turn; to **work lps off hook,** yo, draw through 1 lp on hook (a), (yo, draw through 2 lps on hook) across, leaving 1 lp on hook at end of row (b).

Row 2: Skip 1st vertical bar; for **afghan stitch,** insert hook under next vertical bar (c), yo, draw up ¼" lp; afghan st in each vertical bar across to last vertical bar; for **last st,** insert hook under last bar and st directly behind it (d), yo, draw up ¼" lp; work lps off hook.

For increase, draw up ¼" lp under 1st vertical bar.

For decrease, insert hook under next 2 vertical bars, yo, draw through both bars.

Changing Colors

— Chain Color Change —

(ch color change)
Yo with 2nd color, draw
through last lp on hook.

— Single Crochet Color Change —

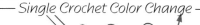

(sc color change)
Drop first color; yo with 2nd color,
draw through last 2 lps of st.

— Half Double Crochet Color Change —

(hdc color change)
Drop first color; yo with 2nd color,
draw through last 3 lps of st.

— Double Crochet Color Change —

(dc color change)
Drop first color; yo with 2nd color,
draw through last 2 lps of st.

Decreasing

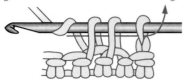

Single Crochet next 2 stitches together	Half Double Crochet next 2 stitches together

(sc next 2 sts tog)
Draw up lp in each of next 2 sts, yo, draw through all 3 lps on hook.

(hdc next 2 sts tog)
(Yo, insert hook in next st, yo, draw lp through) 2 times, yo, draw through all 5 lps on hook.

Double Crochet next 2 stitches together

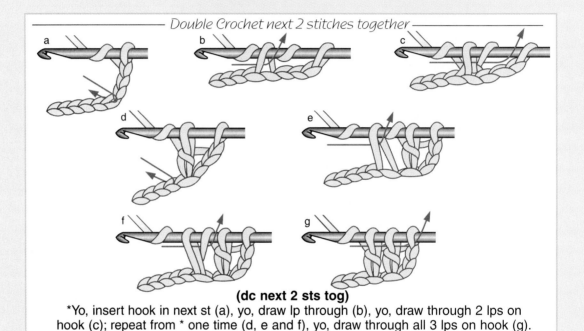

(dc next 2 sts tog)
*Yo, insert hook in next st (a), yo, draw lp through (b), yo, draw through 2 lps on hook (c); repeat from * one time (d, e and f), yo, draw through all 3 lps on hook (g).

Special Stitches

Front Post/Back Post Stitches

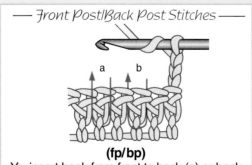

(fp/bp)
Yo, insert hook from front to back (a) or back to front (b) around post of st on previous row; complete as stated in pattern.

Reverse Single Crochet

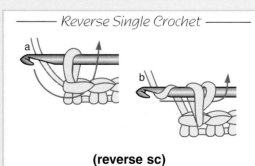

(reverse sc)
Working from left to right, insert hook in next st to the right (a), yo, draw through st, complete as sc (b).

Index